THE INCREDIBLE HULK

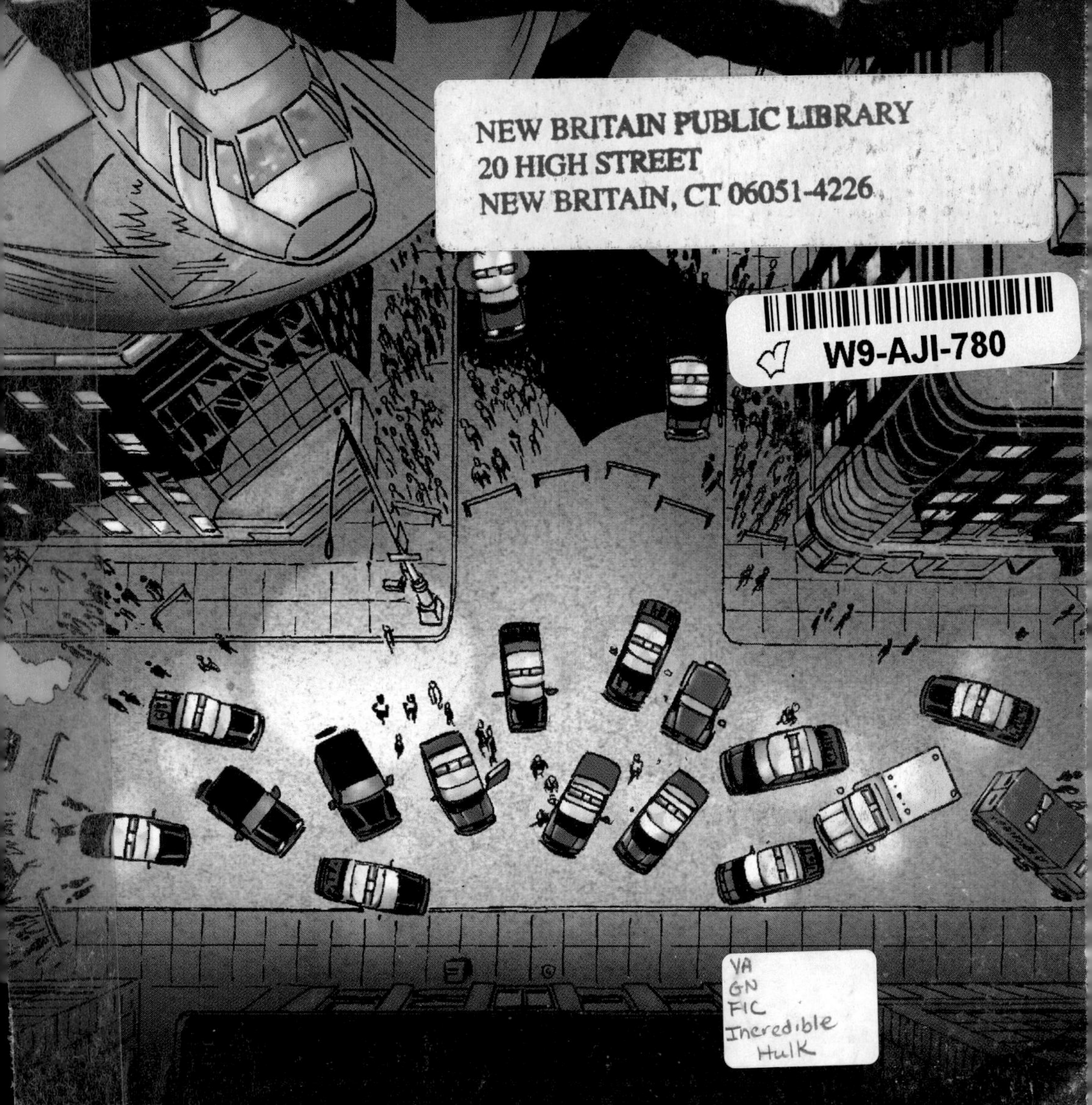

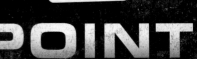

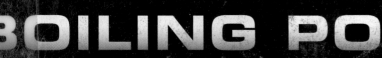

BOILING POINT

THE INCREDIBLE
HULK
BOILING POINT

WRITTEN BY
BRUCE JONES

PENCILS
LEE WEEKS

INKS
TOM PALMER

COLORS
STUDIO F

LETTERS
RS & COMICRAFT'S
WES ABBOTT

COVER
KAARE ANDREWS

EDITOR
AXEL ALONSO

ASSISTANT EDITOR
JOHN MIESEGAES

EDITOR IN CHIEF
JOE QUESADA

PRESIDENT
BILL JEMAS

INCREDIBLE HULK VOL. 2: BOILING POINT. Contains material originally published in magazine form as INCREDIBLE HULK #40-43. Second printing 2002. ISBN# 0-7851-0905-6. Published by MARVEL COMICS, a division of MARVEL ENTERTAINMENT GROUP, INC. OFFICE OF PUBLICATION: 10 East 40th Street, New York, NY 10016. Copyright © 2002 Marvel Characters, Inc. All rights reserved. $8.99 per copy in the U.S. and $14.50 in Canada (GST #R127032852); Canadian Agreement #40668537. All characters featured in this issue and the distinctive names and likenesses thereof, and all related indicia are trademarks of Marvel

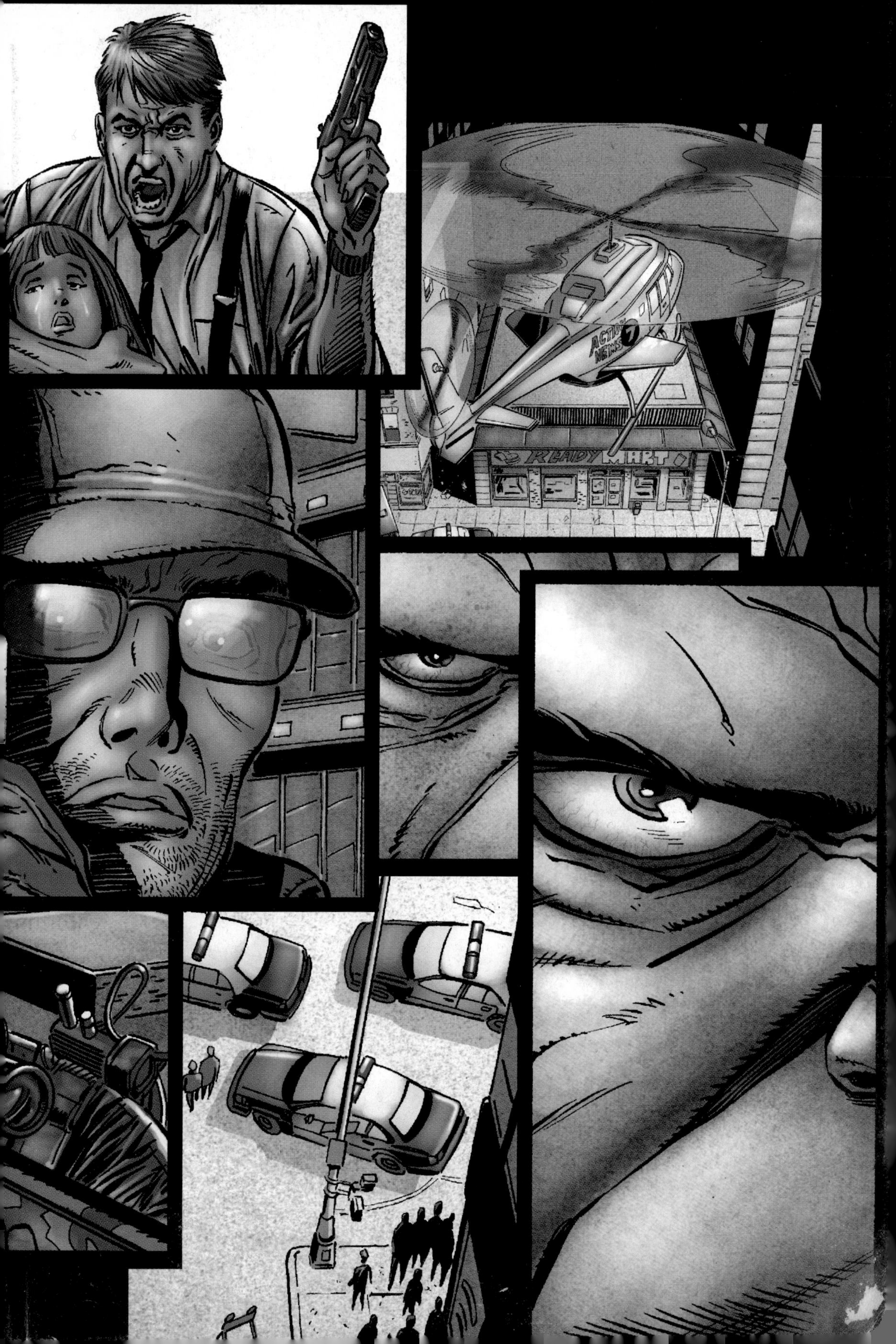
READY MART

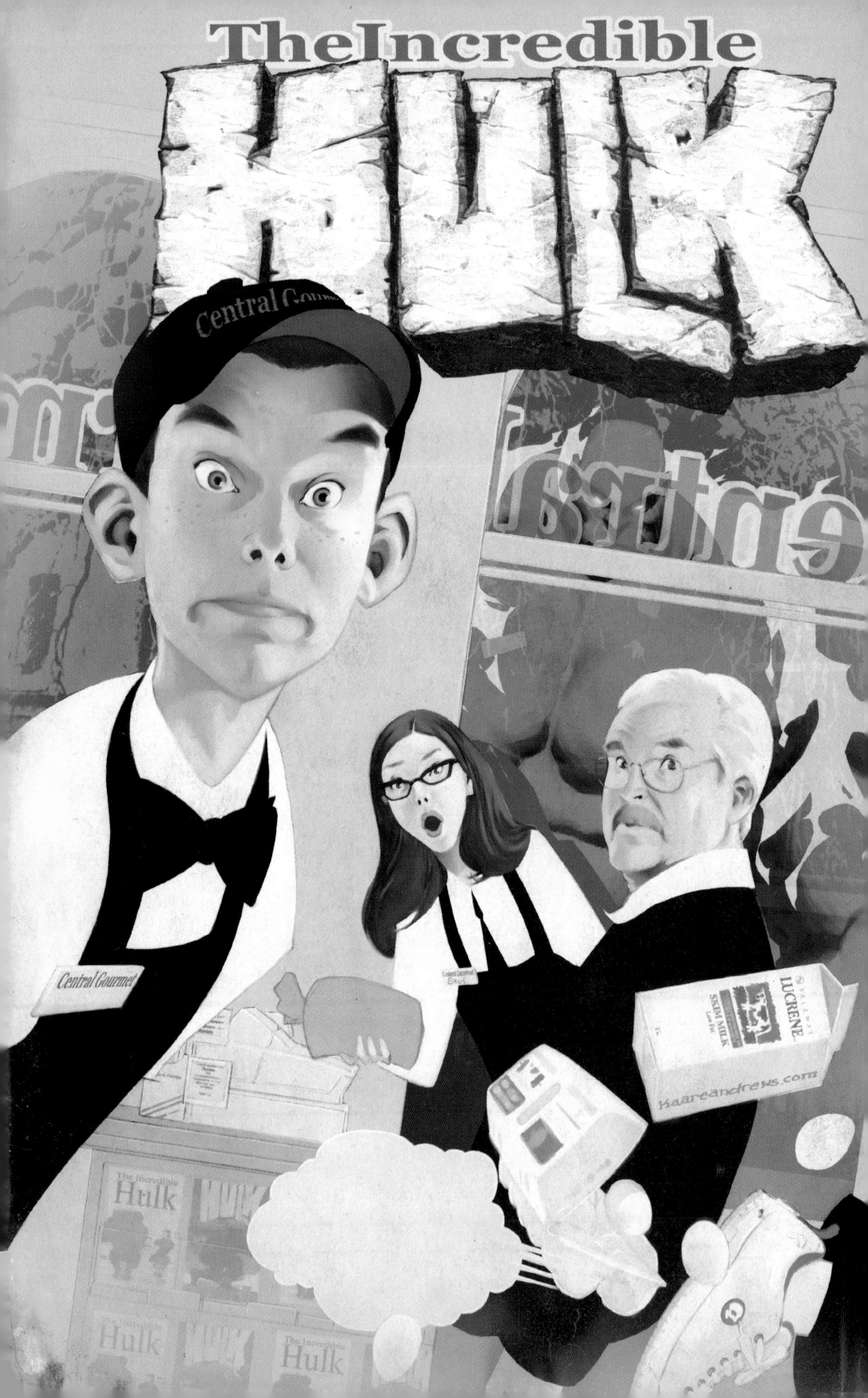
The Incredible
HULK
Central Gourmet
Central Gourmet
LUCRENE
SKIM HULK
Low Fat
kaareandrews.com
The Incredible
Hulk
The Incredible
Hulk
The Incredible
Hulk

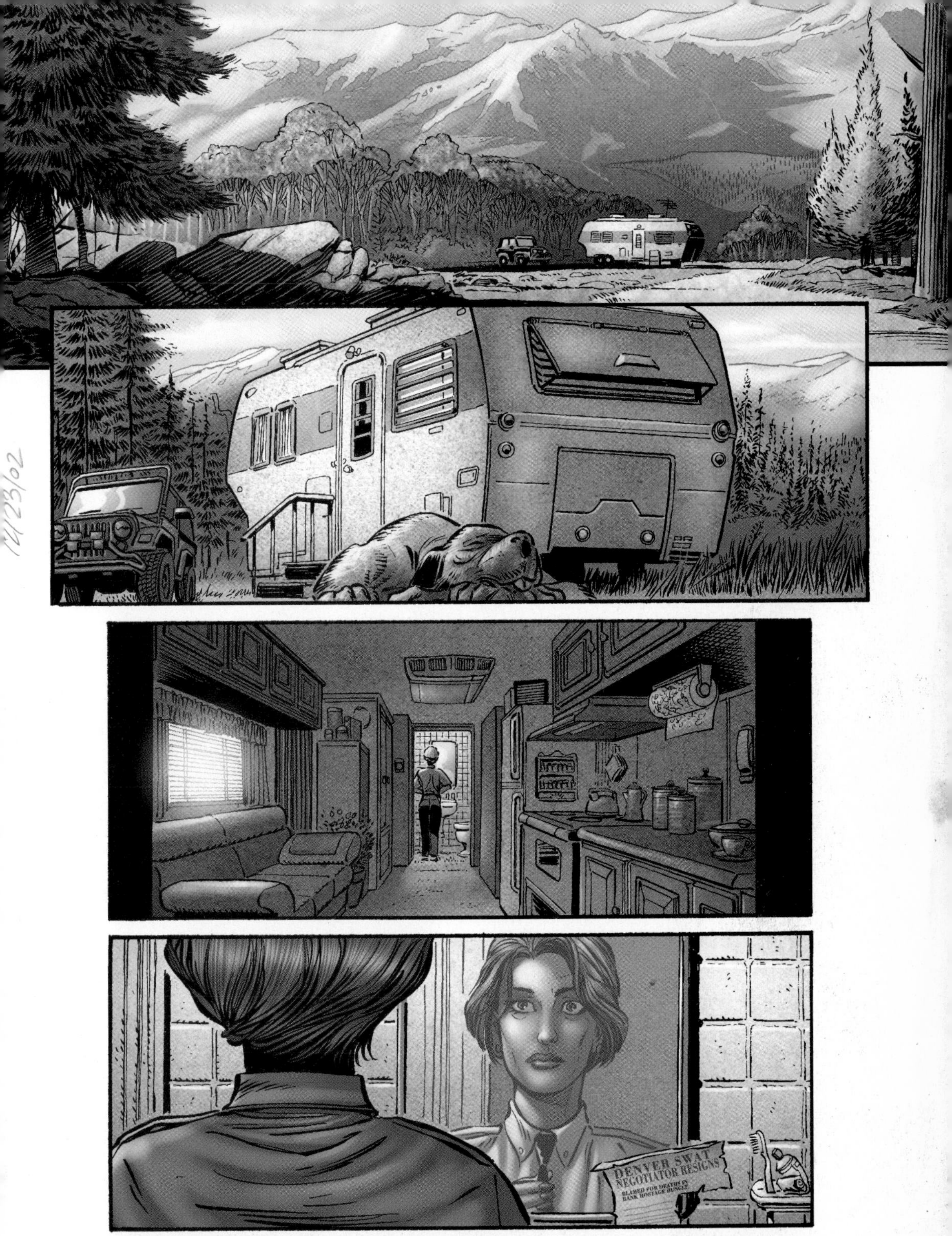
DENVER SWAT
NEGOTIATOR RESIGNS
BLAMED FOR DEATHS IN
BANK HOSTAGE BUNGLE

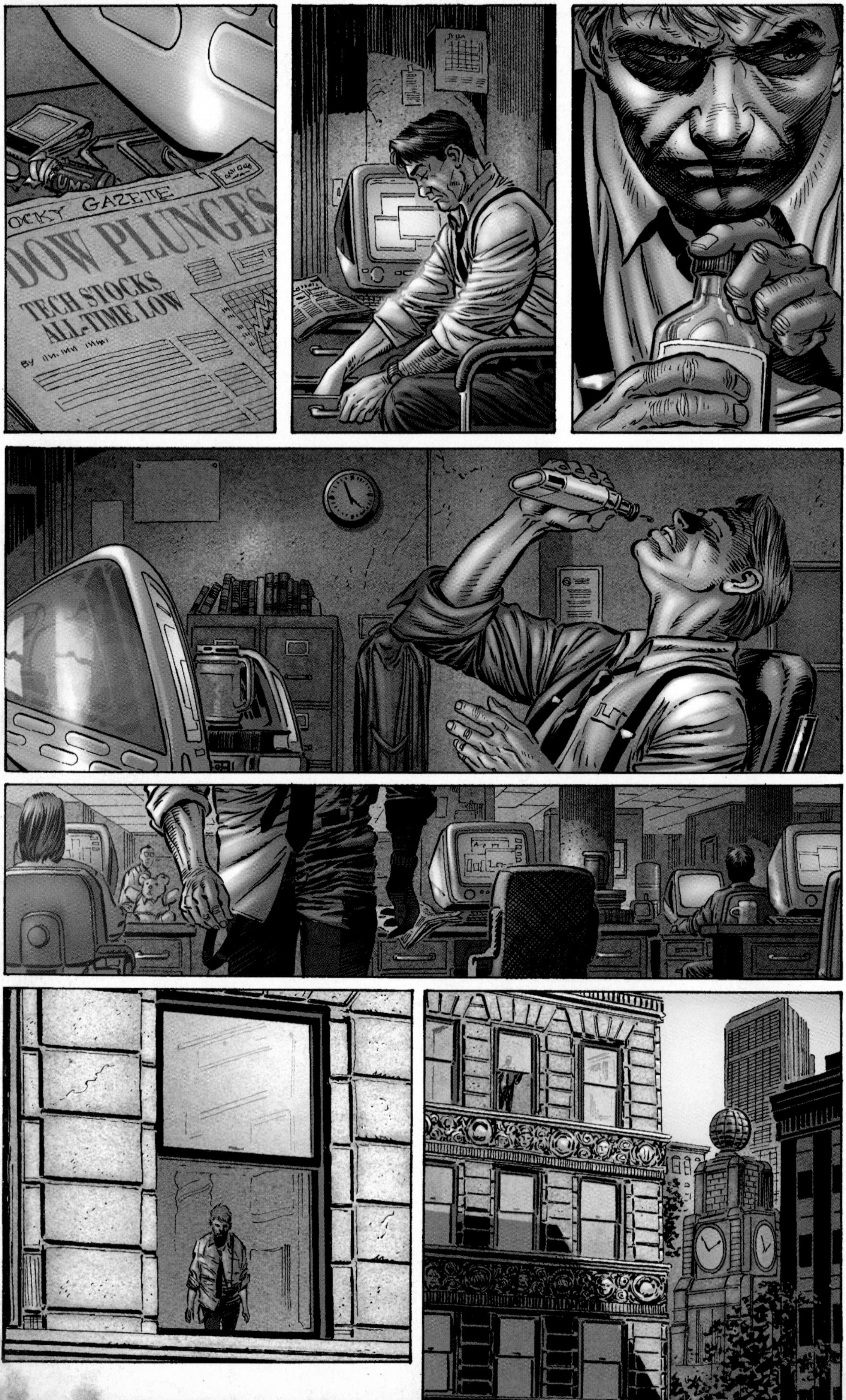

OCKY GAZETTE
DOW PLUNGES
TECH STOCKS ALL-TIME LOW

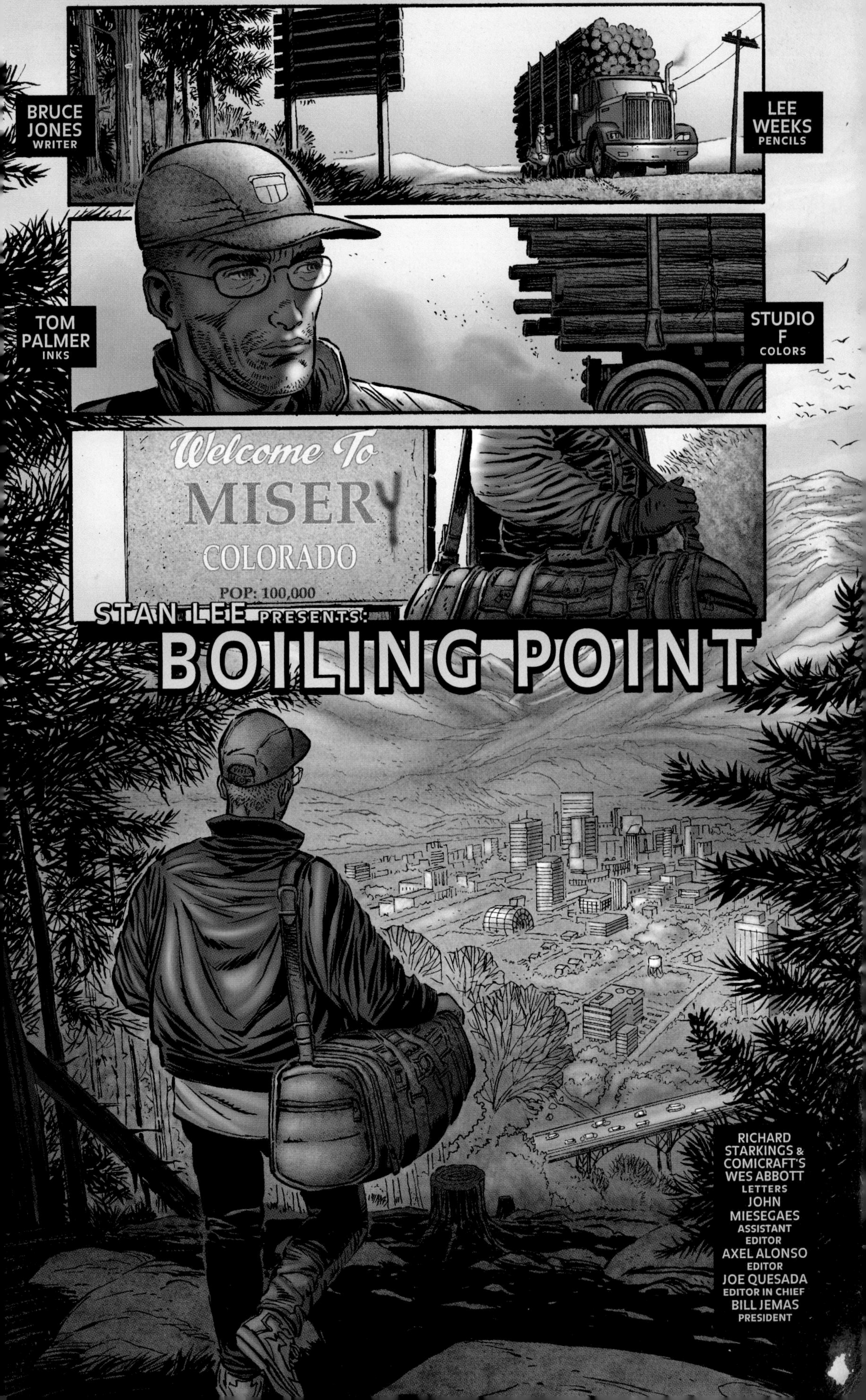

BRUCE JONES WRITER
LEE WEEKS PENCILS
TOM PALMER INKS
STUDIO F COLORS
Welcome To
MISERY
COLORADO
POP: 100,000
STAN LEE PRESENTS:
BOILING POINT
RICHARD STARKINGS & COMICRAFT'S WES ABBOTT LETTERS
JOHN MIESEGAES ASSISTANT EDITOR
AXEL ALONSO EDITOR
JOE QUESADA EDITOR IN CHIEF
BILL JEMAS PRESIDENT

DPD

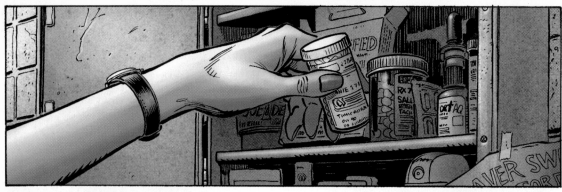

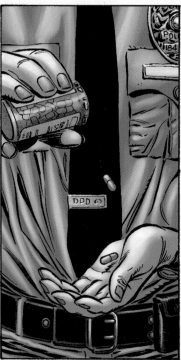

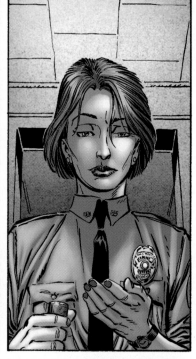

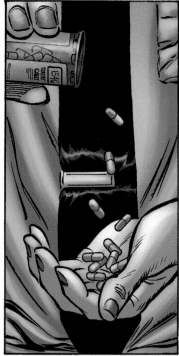

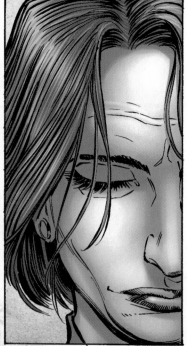

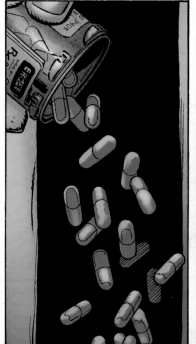

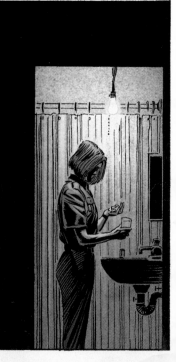

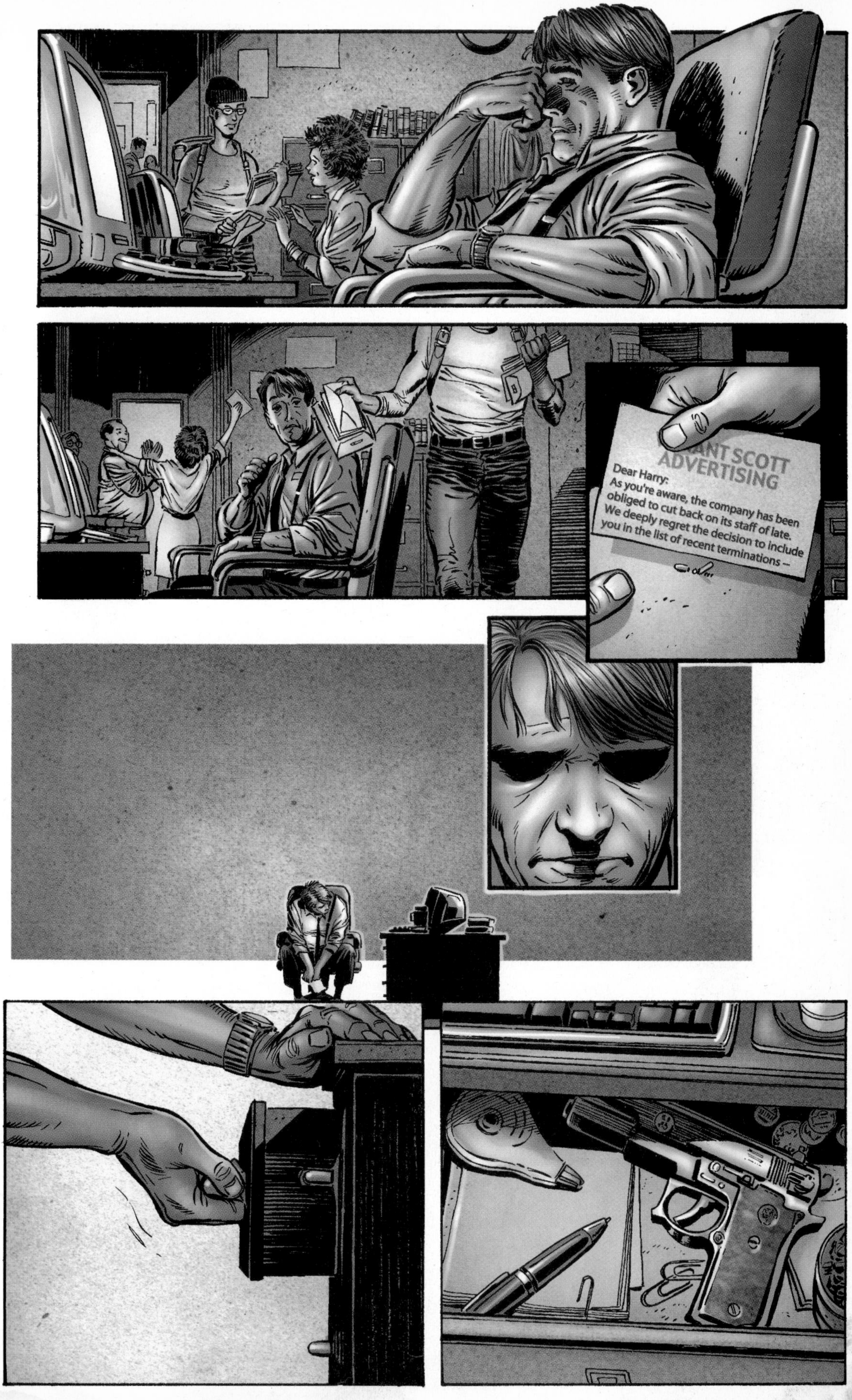
ANT SCOTT ADVERTISING
Dear Harry:
As you're aware, the company has been obliged to cut back on its staff of late. We deeply regret the decision to include you in the list of recent terminations --

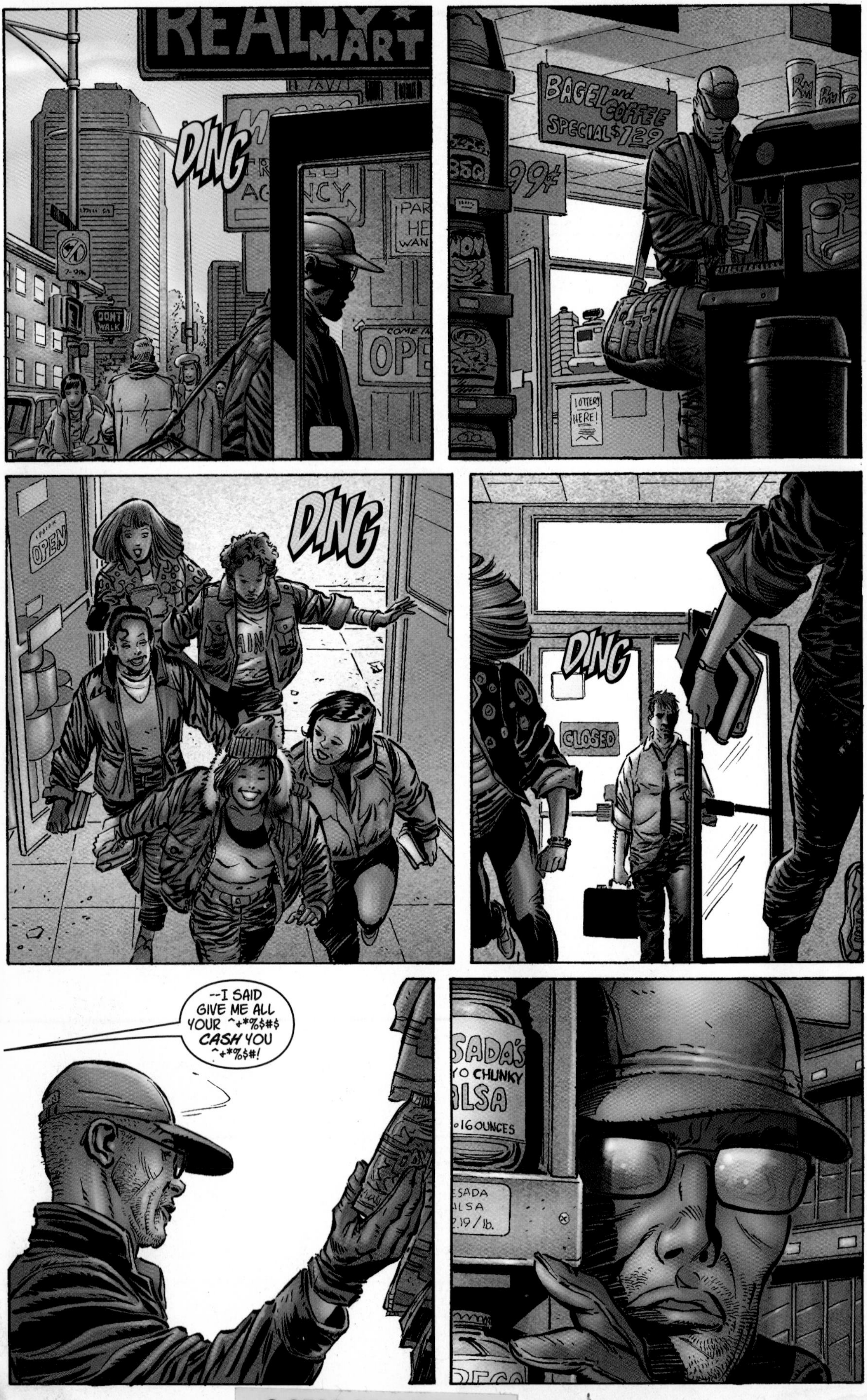
READY MART
DING
AGENCY
DONT WALK
OPEN
BAGEL and COFFEE SPECIAL $1.29
99¢
LOTTERY HERE!
OPEN
DING
DING
CLOSED
--I SAID GIVE ME ALL YOUR ^+*%$#$ *CASH* YOU ^+*%$#!
CHUNKY
16 OUNCES

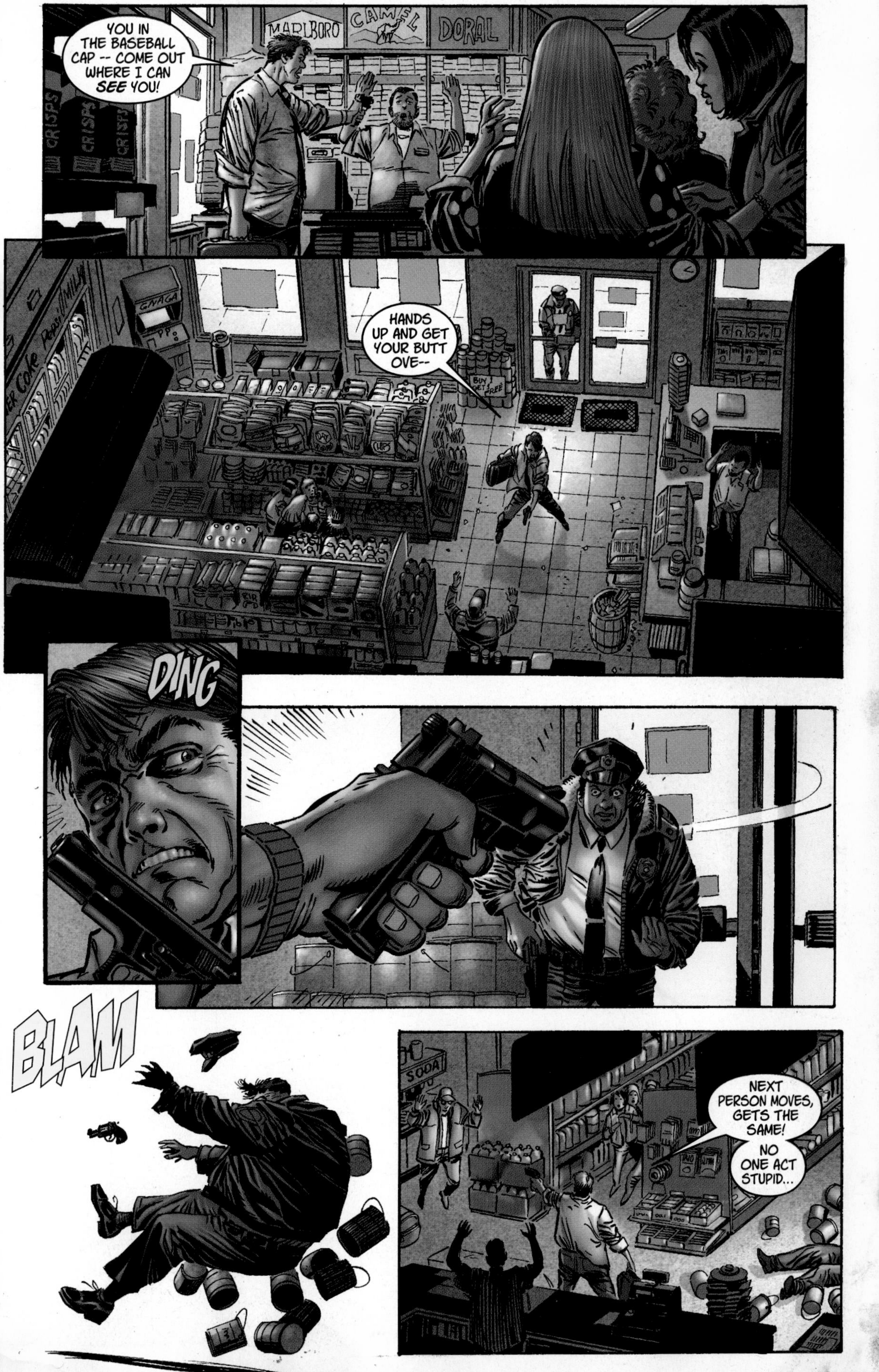

MARLBORO
CAMEL
DORAL
CRISPS
YOU IN THE BASEBALL CAP -- COME OUT WHERE I CAN SEE YOU!
HANDS UP AND GET YOUR BUTT OVE--
SODA
DING
BLAM
NEXT PERSON MOVES, GETS THE SAME!
NO ONE ACT STUPID...

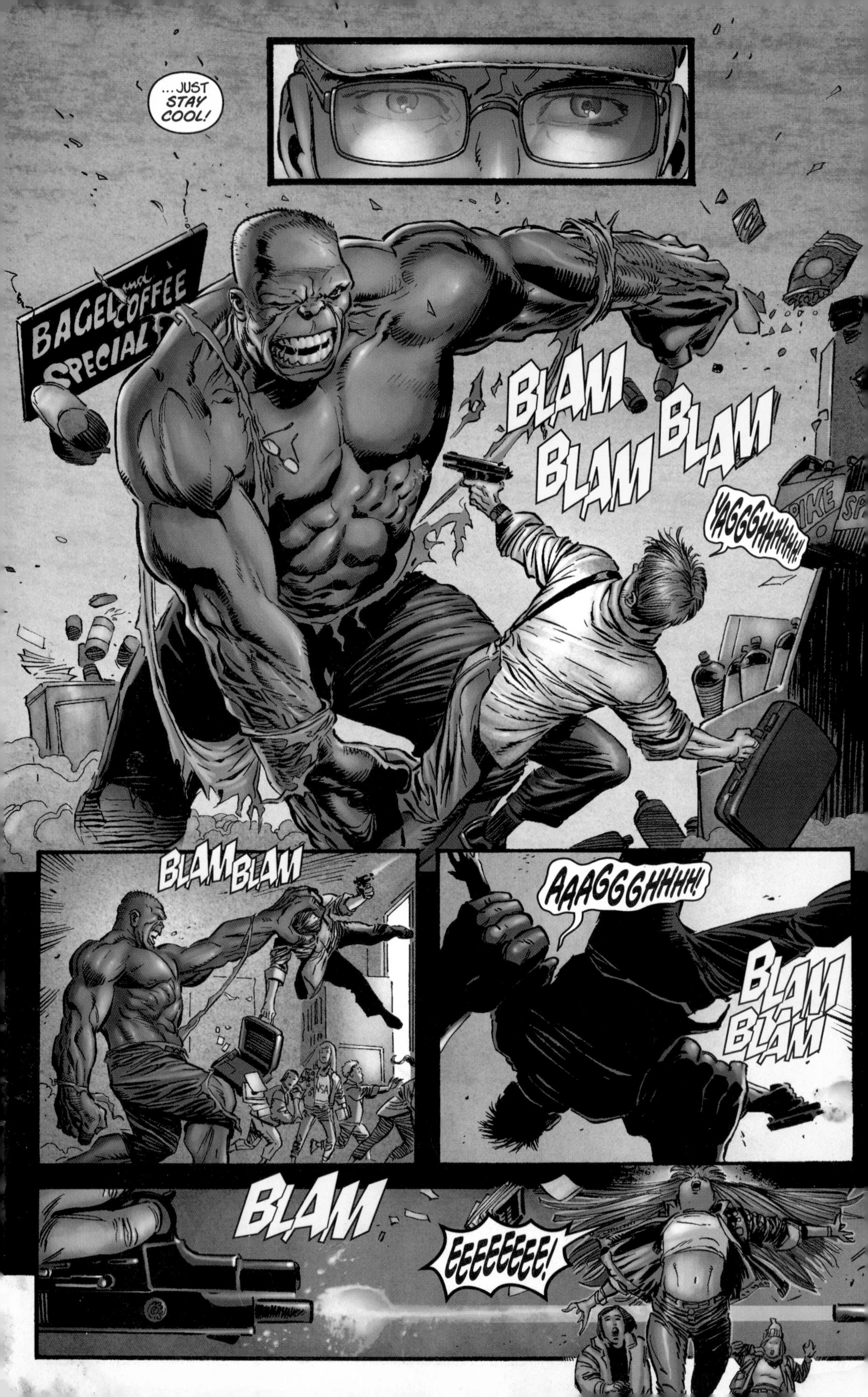
...JUST STAY COOL!
BAGEL and COFFEE SPECIAL
BLAM
BLAM BLAM BLAM
YAGGGHHHHH!
BLAMBLAM
AAAGGGHHHH!
BLAM BLAM
BLAM
EEEEEEEE!

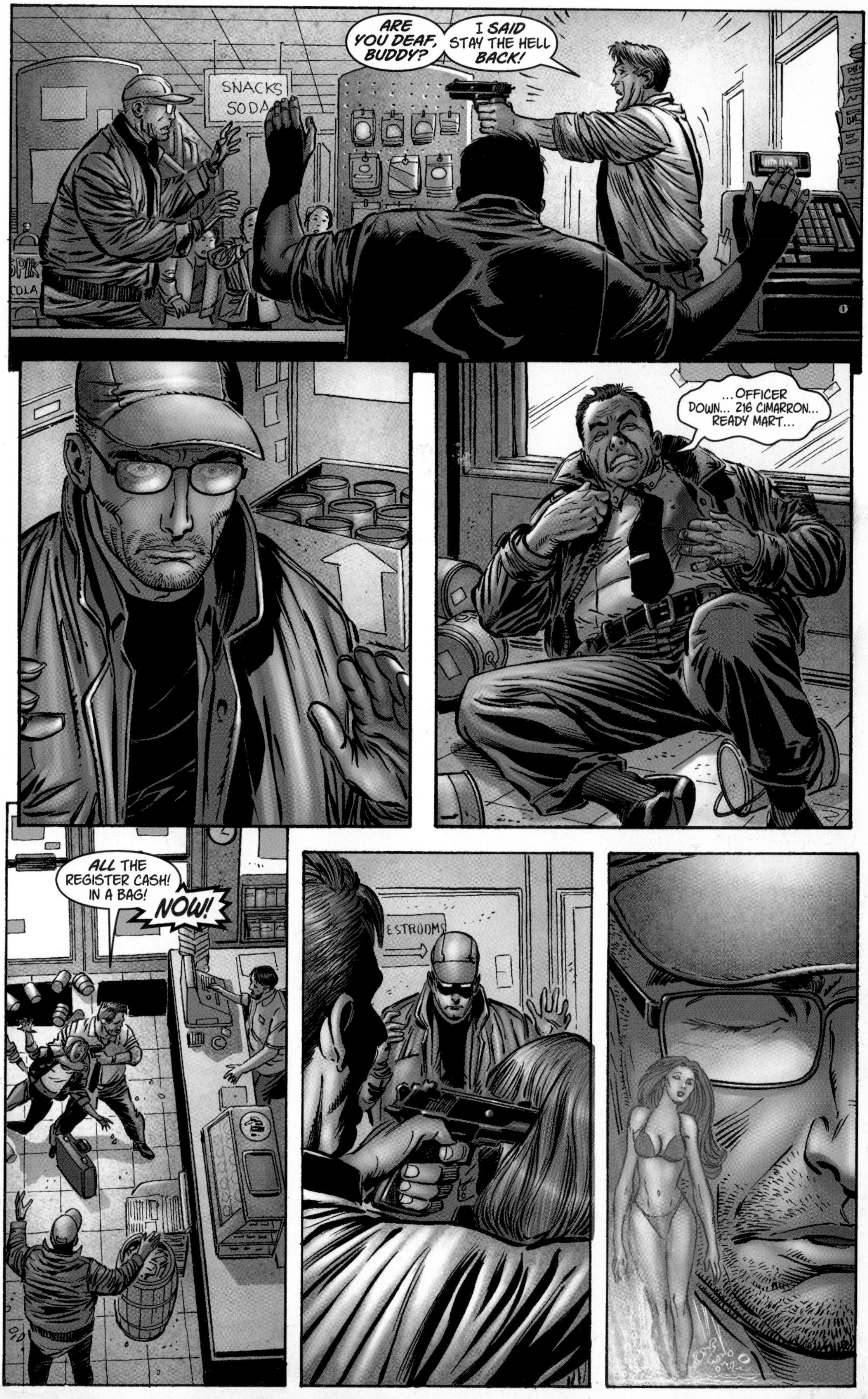
ARE YOU DEAF, BUDDY?
I SAID STAY THE HELL BACK!
SNACKS
SODA
...OFFICER DOWN... 216 CIMARRON... READY MART...
ALL THE REGISTER CASH! IN A BAG!
NOW!
ESTROOMS

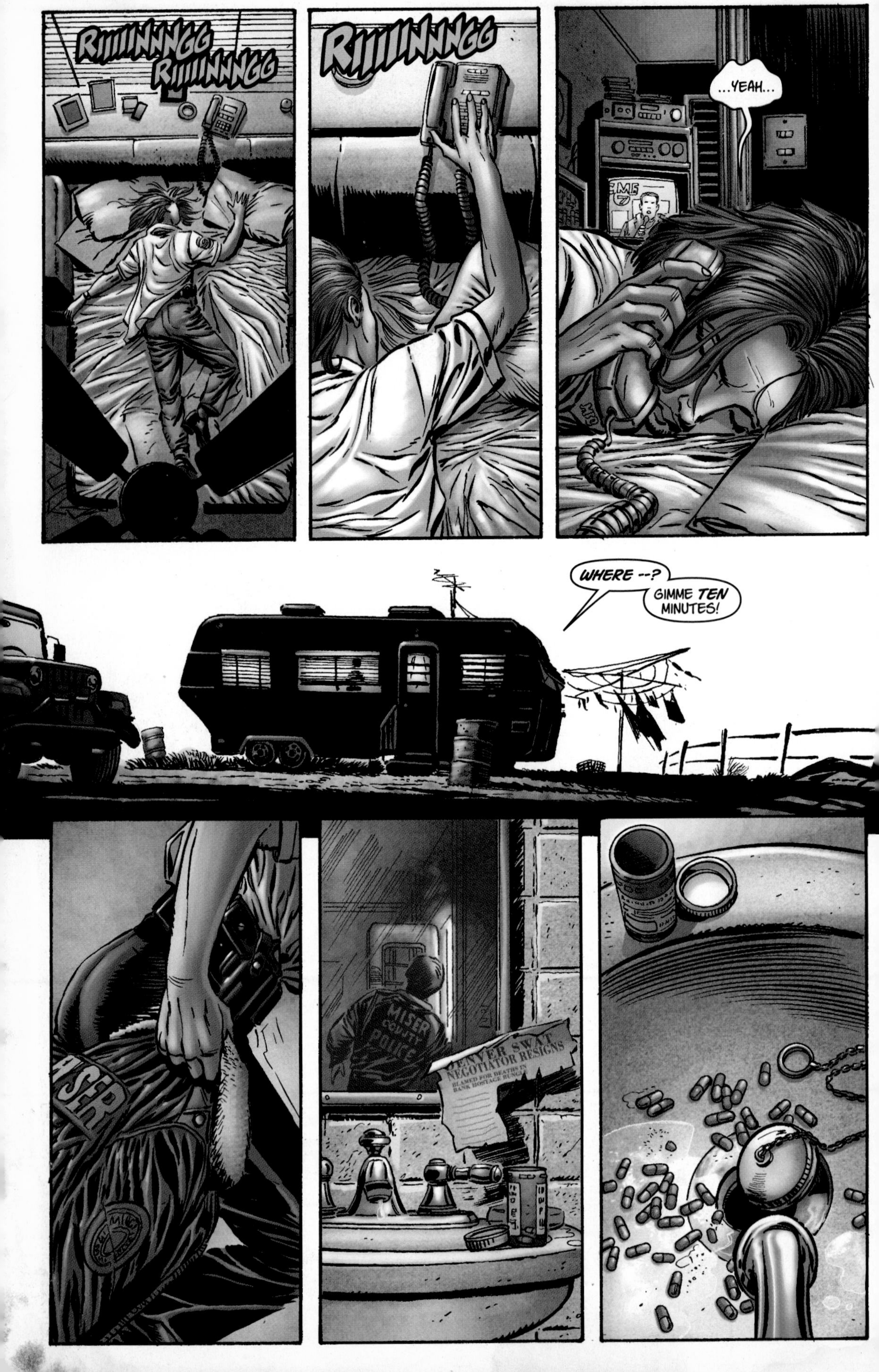
RIIIINNNGG
RIIIINNNGG
RIIIINNNGG
...YEAH...
WHERE --?
GIMME TEN MINUTES!
MISER COUNTY POLICE
DENVER SWAT NEGOTIATOR RESIGNS

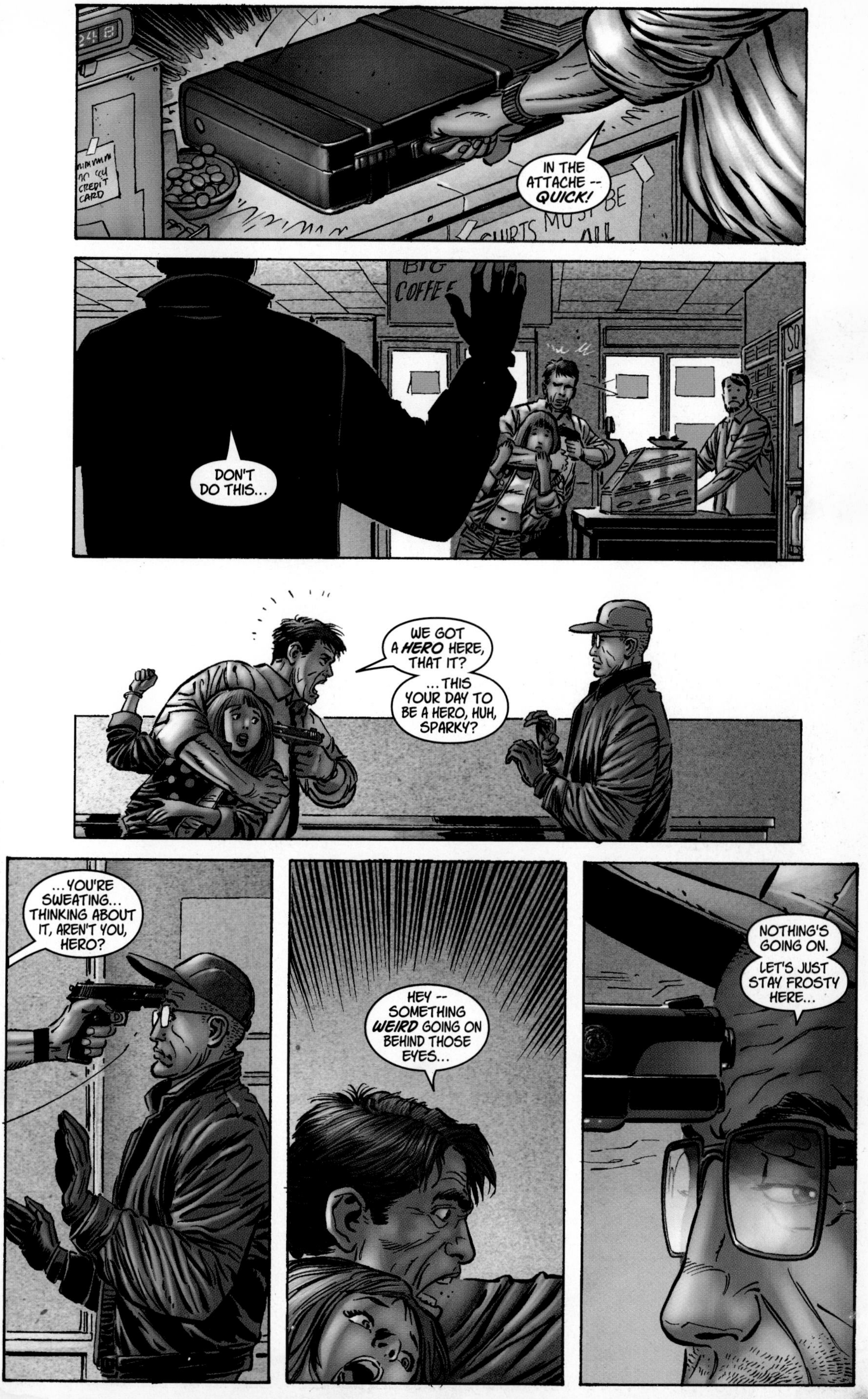
IN THE ATTACHE -- QUICK!
DON'T DO THIS...
WE GOT A HERO HERE, THAT IT?
...THIS YOUR DAY TO BE A HERO, HUH, SPARKY?
...YOU'RE SWEATING... THINKING ABOUT IT, AREN'T YOU, HERO?
HEY -- SOMETHING WEIRD GOING ON BEHIND THOSE EYES...
NOTHING'S GOING ON.
LET'S JUST STAY FROSTY HERE...

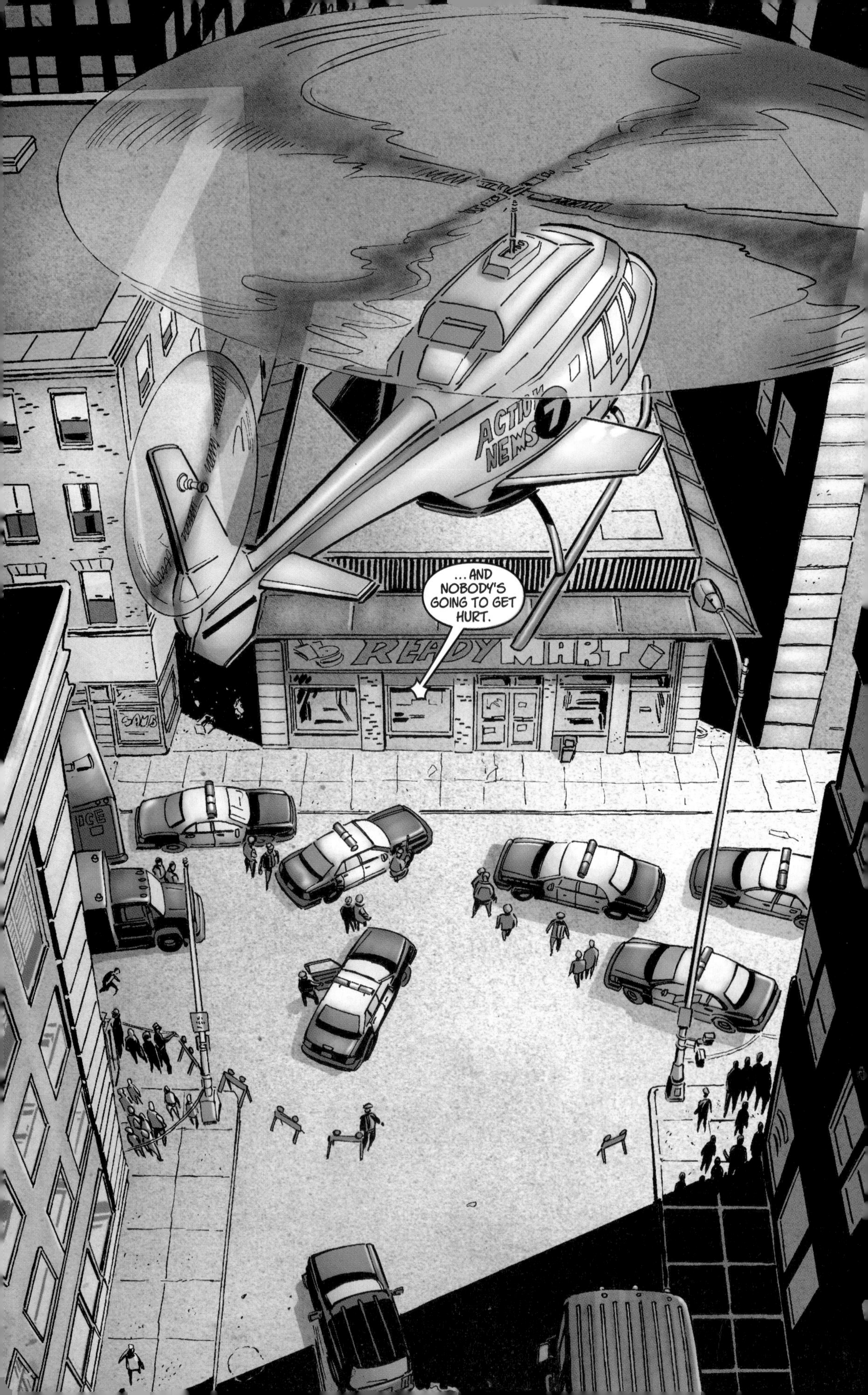
...AND NOBODY'S GOING TO GET HURT.
ACTION NEWS 7
READY MART

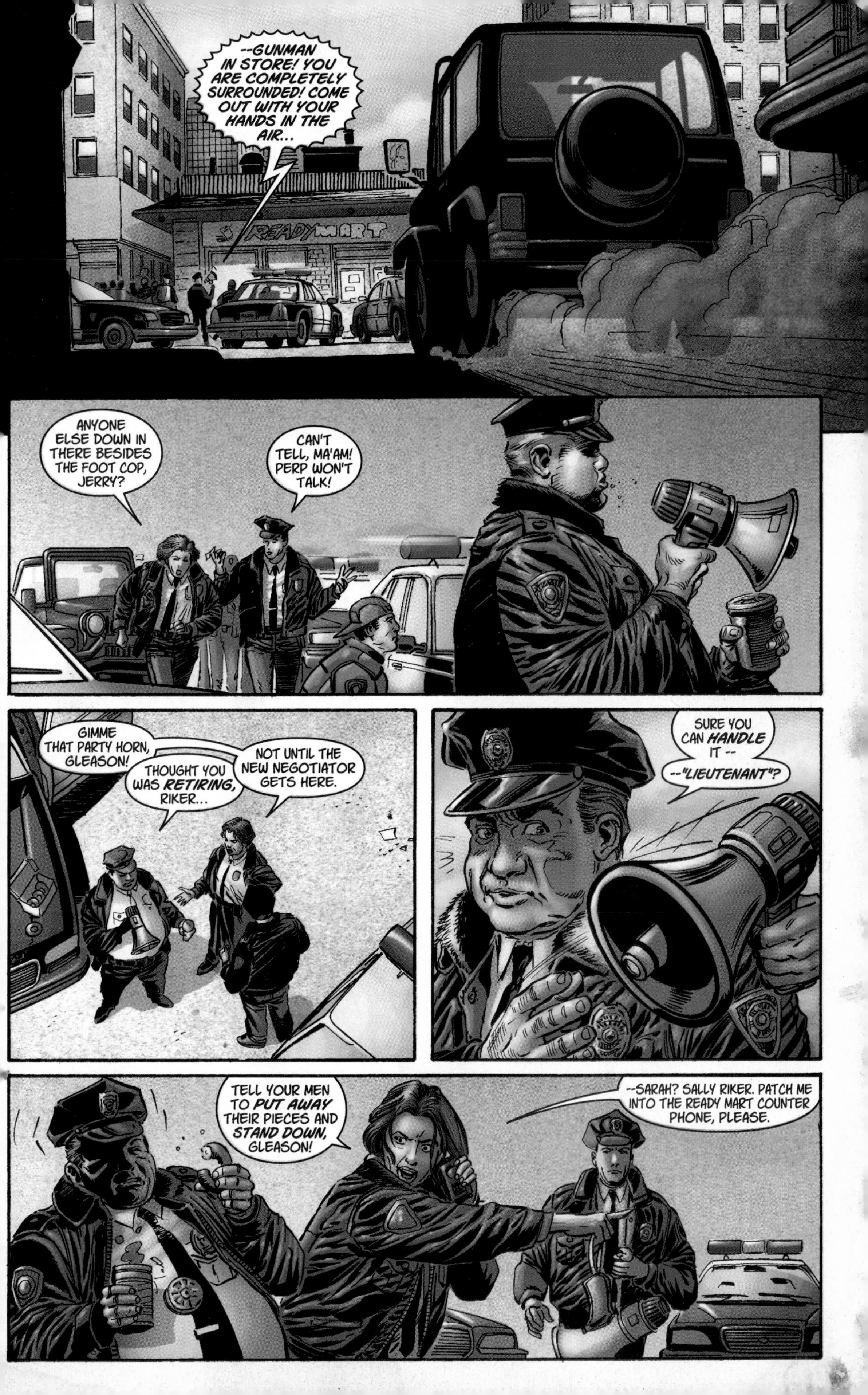
--GUNMAN IN STORE! YOU ARE COMPLETELY SURROUNDED! COME OUT WITH YOUR HANDS IN THE AIR...
READYMART
ANYONE ELSE DOWN IN THERE BESIDES THE FOOT COP, JERRY?
CAN'T TELL, MA'AM! PERP WON'T TALK!
GIMME THAT PARTY HORN, GLEASON!
THOUGHT YOU WAS RETIRING, RIKER...
NOT UNTIL THE NEW NEGOTIATOR GETS HERE.
SURE YOU CAN HANDLE IT --
--"LIEUTENANT"?
TELL YOUR MEN TO PUT AWAY THEIR PIECES AND STAND DOWN, GLEASON!
--SARAH? SALLY RIKER. PATCH ME INTO THE READY MART COUNTER PHONE, PLEASE.

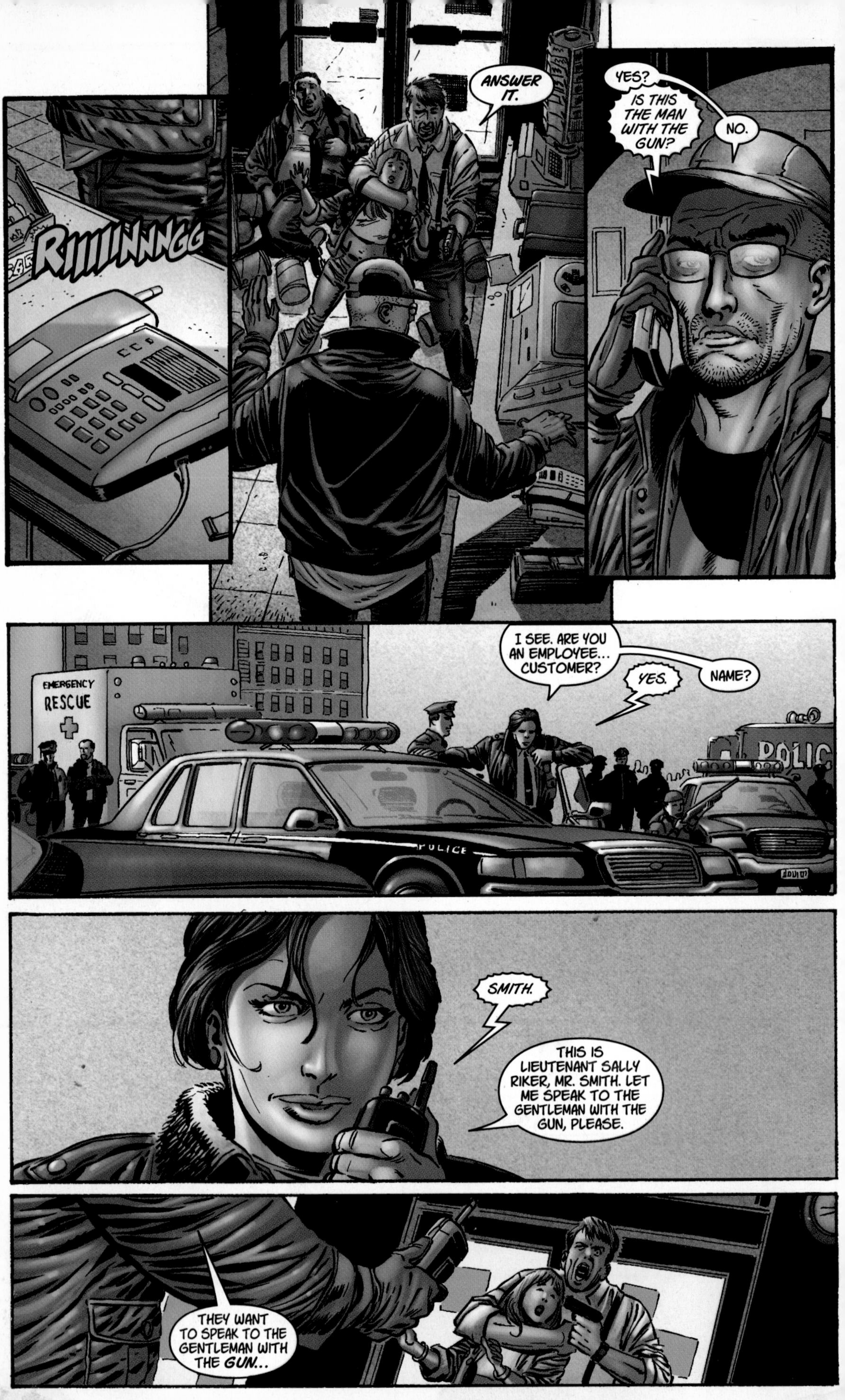
RIIIINNNGG
ANSWER IT.
YES?
IS THIS THE MAN WITH THE GUN?
NO.
I SEE. ARE YOU AN EMPLOYEE... CUSTOMER?
YES.
NAME?
EMERGENCY RESCUE
POLICE
POLIC
SMITH.
THIS IS LIEUTENANT SALLY RIKER, MR. SMITH. LET ME SPEAK TO THE GENTLEMAN WITH THE GUN, PLEASE.
THEY WANT TO SPEAK TO THE GENTLEMAN WITH THE GUN...

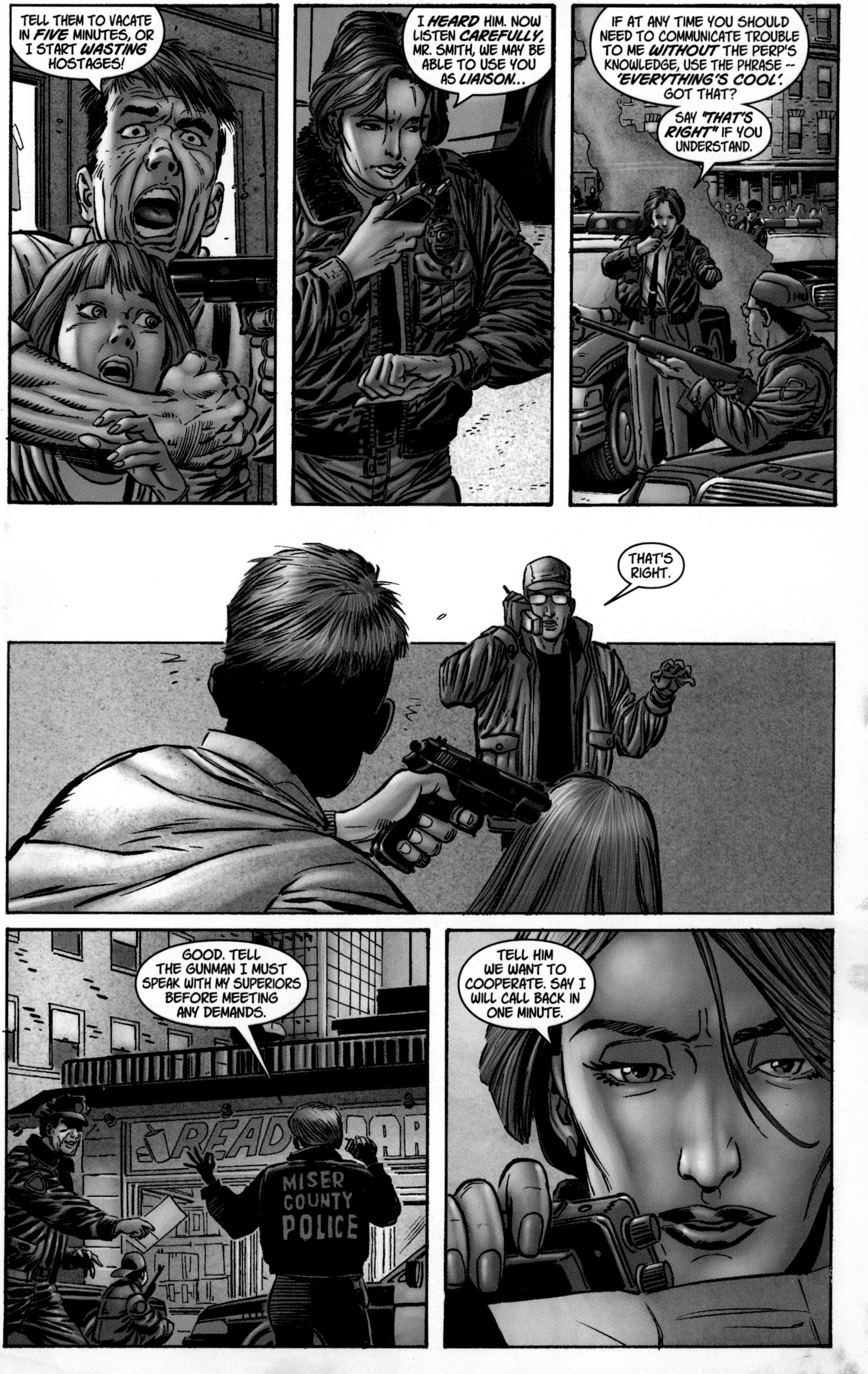
TELL THEM TO VACATE IN FIVE MINUTES, OR I START WASTING HOSTAGES!
I HEARD HIM. NOW LISTEN CAREFULLY, MR. SMITH, WE MAY BE ABLE TO USE YOU AS LIAISON...
IF AT ANY TIME YOU SHOULD NEED TO COMMUNICATE TROUBLE TO ME WITHOUT THE PERP'S KNOWLEDGE, USE THE PHRASE -- 'EVERYTHING'S COOL'. GOT THAT?
SAY "THAT'S RIGHT" IF YOU UNDERSTAND.
THAT'S RIGHT.
GOOD. TELL THE GUNMAN I MUST SPEAK WITH MY SUPERIORS BEFORE MEETING ANY DEMANDS.
MISER COUNTY POLICE
TELL HIM WE WANT TO COOPERATE. SAY I WILL CALL BACK IN ONE MINUTE.

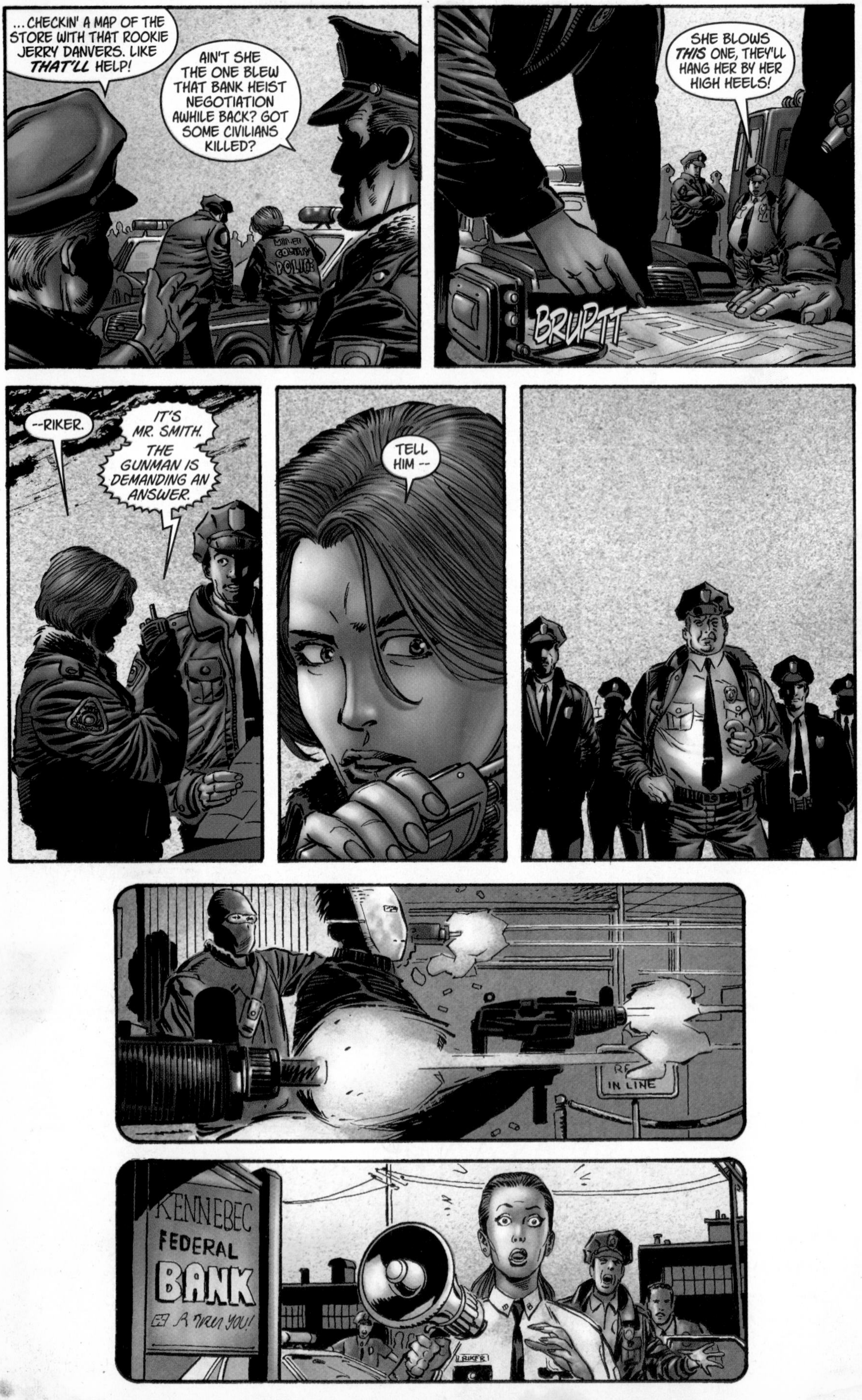

... CHECKIN' A MAP OF THE STORE WITH THAT ROOKIE JERRY DANVERS. LIKE THAT'LL HELP!
AIN'T SHE THE ONE BLEW THAT BANK HEIST NEGOTIATION AWHILE BACK? GOT SOME CIVILIANS KILLED?
SHE BLOWS THIS ONE, THEY'LL HANG HER BY HER HIGH HEELS!
BRUPTT
--RIKER.
IT'S MR. SMITH. THE GUNMAN IS DEMANDING AN ANSWER.
TELL HIM --
IN LINE
KENNEBEC
FEDERAL
BANK
RIKER

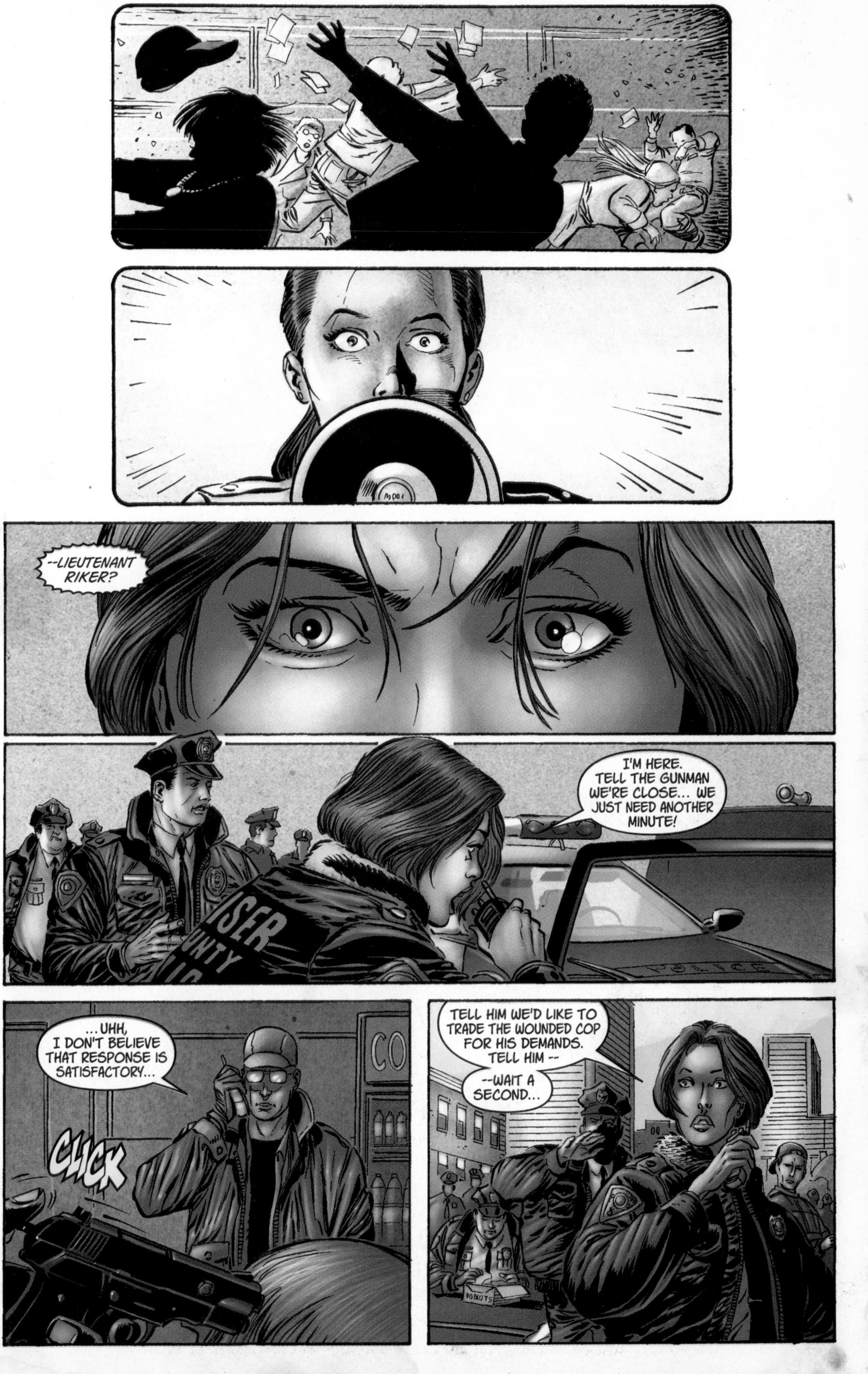
--LIEUTENANT RIKER?
I'M HERE. TELL THE GUNMAN WE'RE CLOSE... WE JUST NEED ANOTHER MINUTE!
...UHH, I DON'T BELIEVE THAT RESPONSE IS SATISFACTORY...
CLICK
TELL HIM WE'D LIKE TO TRADE THE WOUNDED COP FOR HIS DEMANDS. TELL HIM --
--WAIT A SECOND...
DONUTS
POLICE

-- 'SCUSE ME, LIEUTENANT.

HEY... HEY!

WHO THE HELL ARE *YOU?!*

SPECIAL AGENT PRATT, F.B.I.

WE'LL TAKE IT FROM HERE, LIEUTENANT.

DEPARTMENT OF
FBI
SPECIAL AGENT

THIS IS SPECIAL AGENT PRATT. AM I SPEAKING WITH THE CIVILIAN LIAISON?

YES...

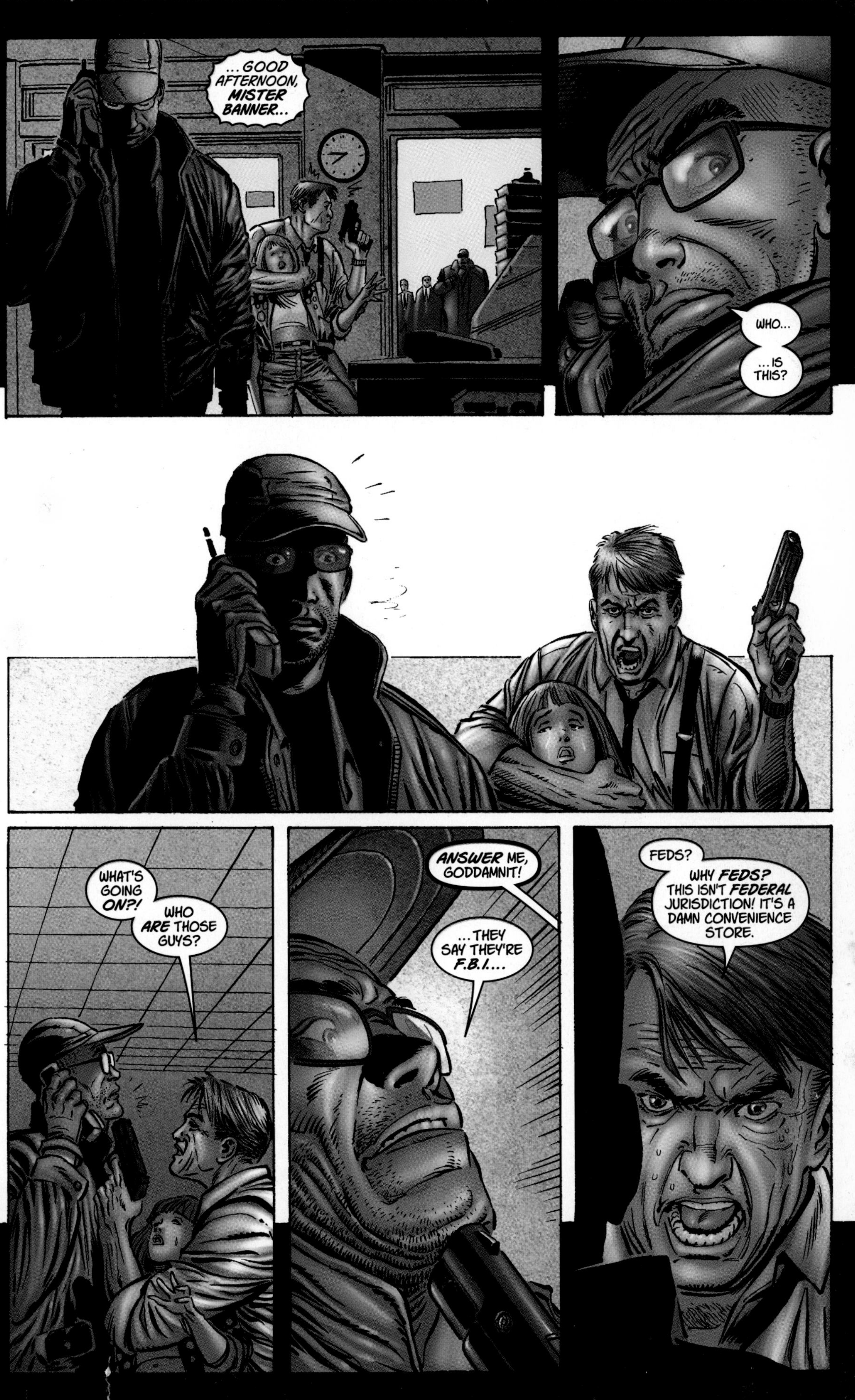
...GOOD AFTERNOON, MISTER BANNER...
WHO...
...IS THIS?
WHAT'S GOING ON?!
WHO ARE THOSE GUYS?
ANSWER ME, GODDAMNIT!
...THEY SAY THEY'RE F.B.I....
FEDS?
WHY FEDS? THIS ISN'T FEDERAL JURISDICTION! IT'S A DAMN CONVENIENCE STORE.

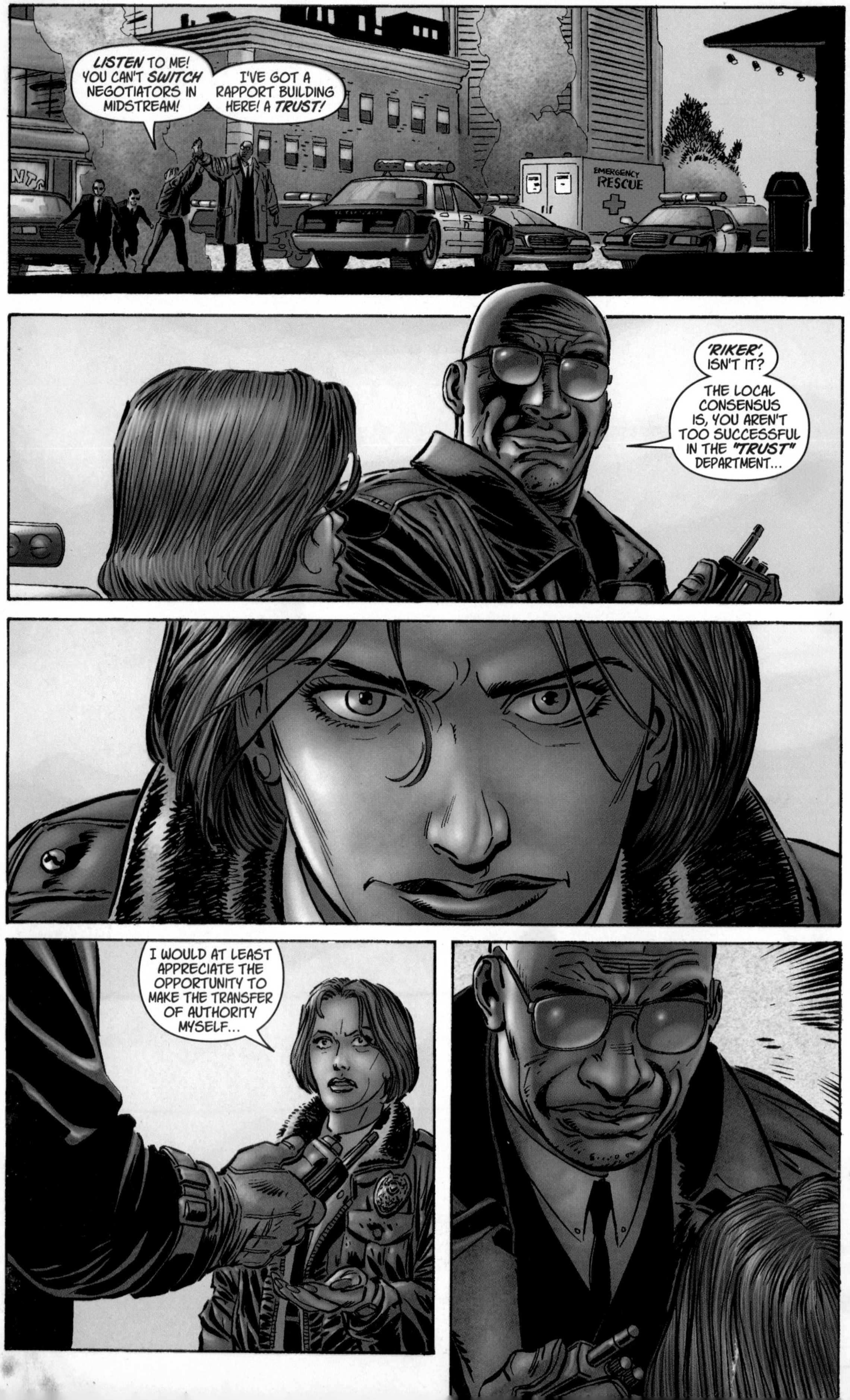
LISTEN TO ME! YOU CAN'T SWITCH NEGOTIATORS IN MIDSTREAM!
I'VE GOT A RAPPORT BUILDING HERE! A TRUST!
EMERGENCY RESCUE
'RIKER', ISN'T IT?
THE LOCAL CONSENSUS IS, YOU AREN'T TOO SUCCESSFUL IN THE "TRUST" DEPARTMENT...
I WOULD AT LEAST APPRECIATE THE OPPORTUNITY TO MAKE THE TRANSFER OF AUTHORITY MYSELF...

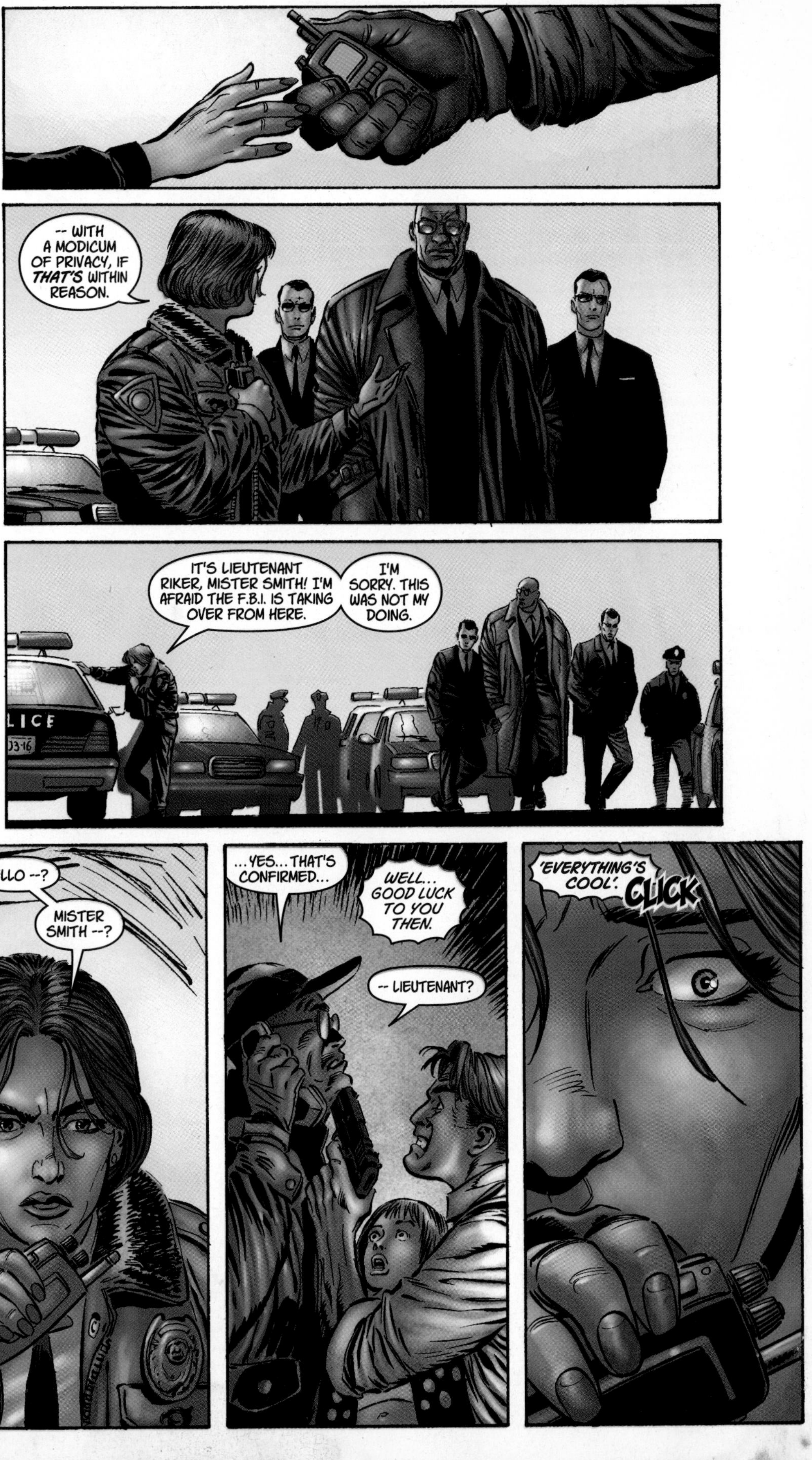
-- WITH A MODICUM OF PRIVACY, IF *THAT'S* WITHIN REASON.
IT'S LIEUTENANT RIKER, MISTER SMITH! I'M AFRAID THE F.B.I. IS TAKING OVER FROM HERE.
I'M SORRY. THIS WAS NOT MY DOING.
LICE
HELLO --?
MISTER SMITH --?
...YES...THAT'S CONFIRMED...
WELL... GOOD LUCK TO YOU THEN.
-- LIEUTENANT?
'EVERYTHING'S COOL'.
CLICK

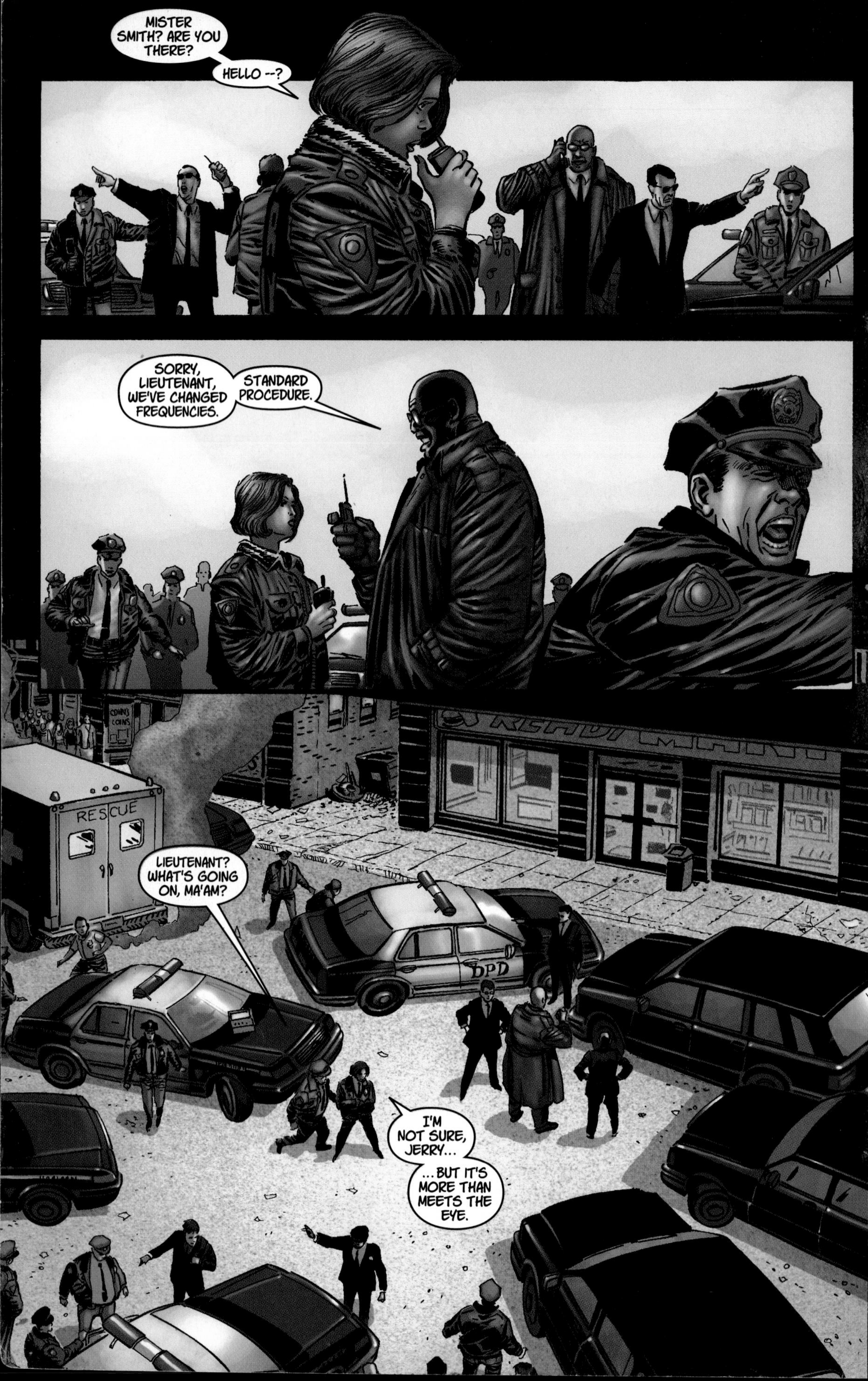
MISTER SMITH? ARE YOU THERE?
HELLO --?
SORRY, LIEUTENANT, WE'VE CHANGED FREQUENCIES.
STANDARD PROCEDURE.
RESCUE
LIEUTENANT? WHAT'S GOING ON, MA'AM?
DPD
I'M NOT SURE, JERRY...
...BUT IT'S MORE THAN MEETS THE EYE.

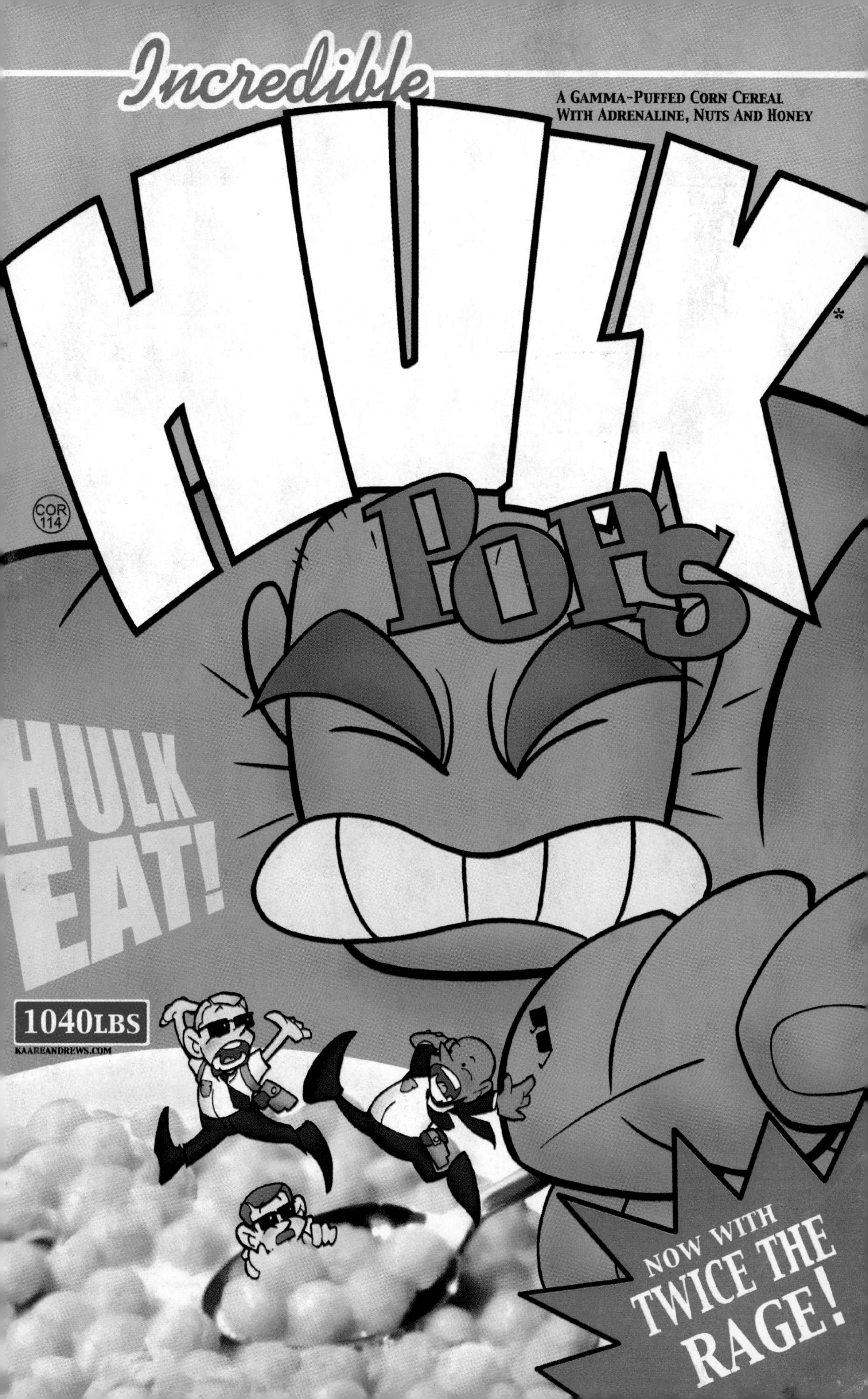
Incredible
A Gamma-Puffed Corn Cereal
With Adrenaline, Nuts And Honey
HULK*
POPS
COR 114
HULK EAT!
1040LBS
KAAREANDREWS.COM
NOW WITH
TWICE THE
RAGE!

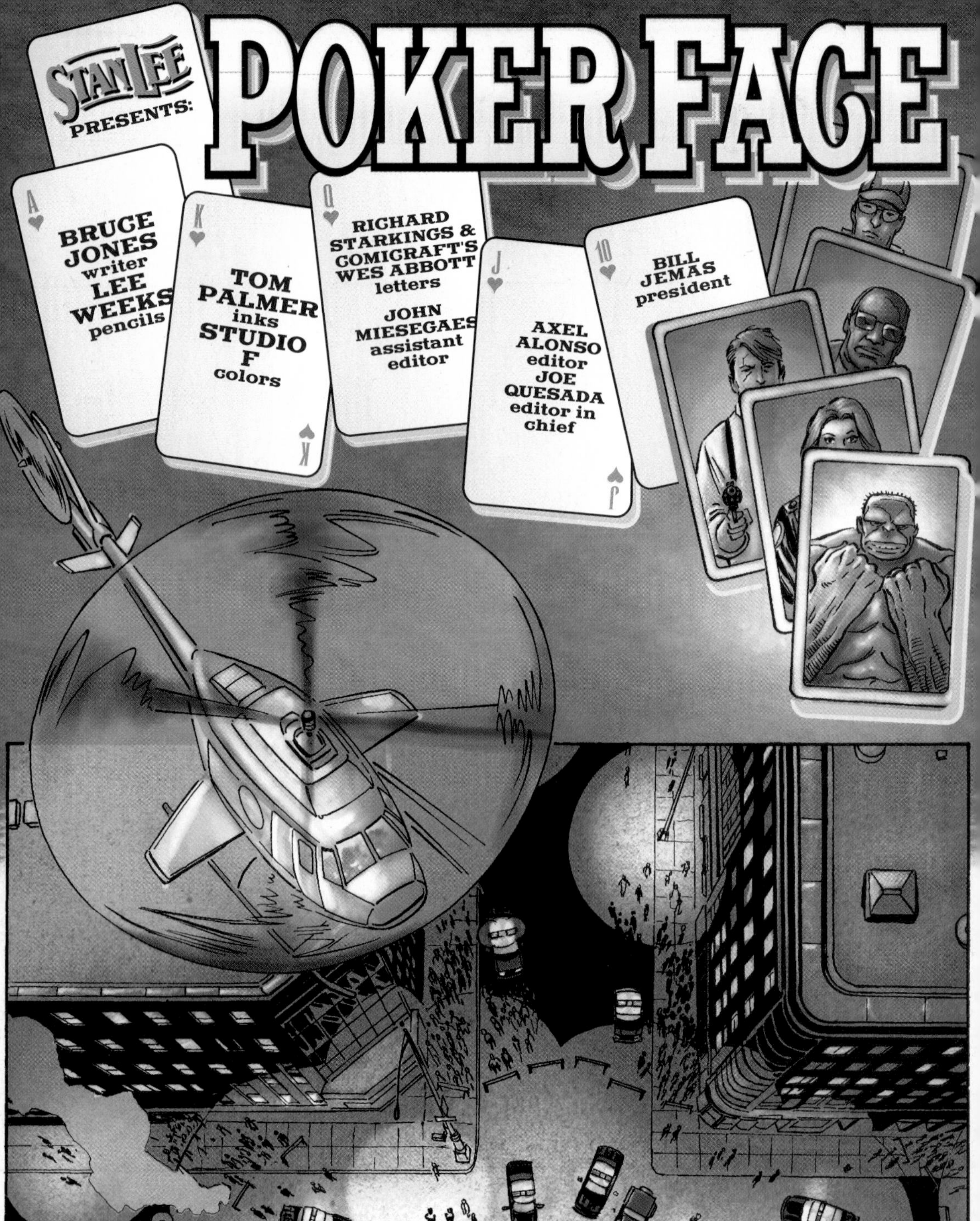
STAN LEE PRESENTS:
POKER FACE
BRUCE JONES writer
LEE WEEKS pencils
TOM PALMER inks
STUDIO F colors
RICHARD STARKINGS & COMICRAFT'S WES ABBOTT letters
JOHN MIESEGAES assistant editor
AXEL ALONSO editor
JOE QUESADA editor in chief
BILL JEMAS president

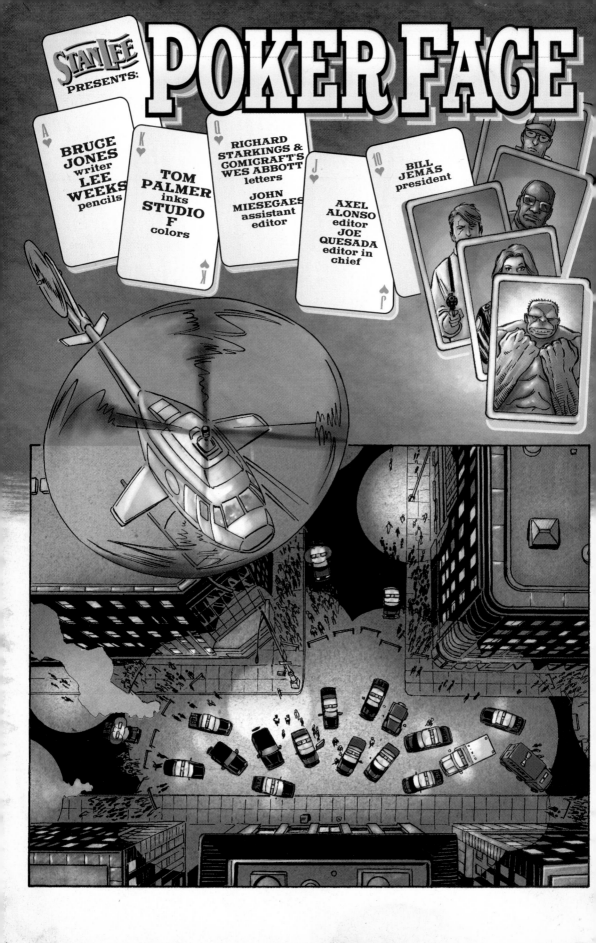

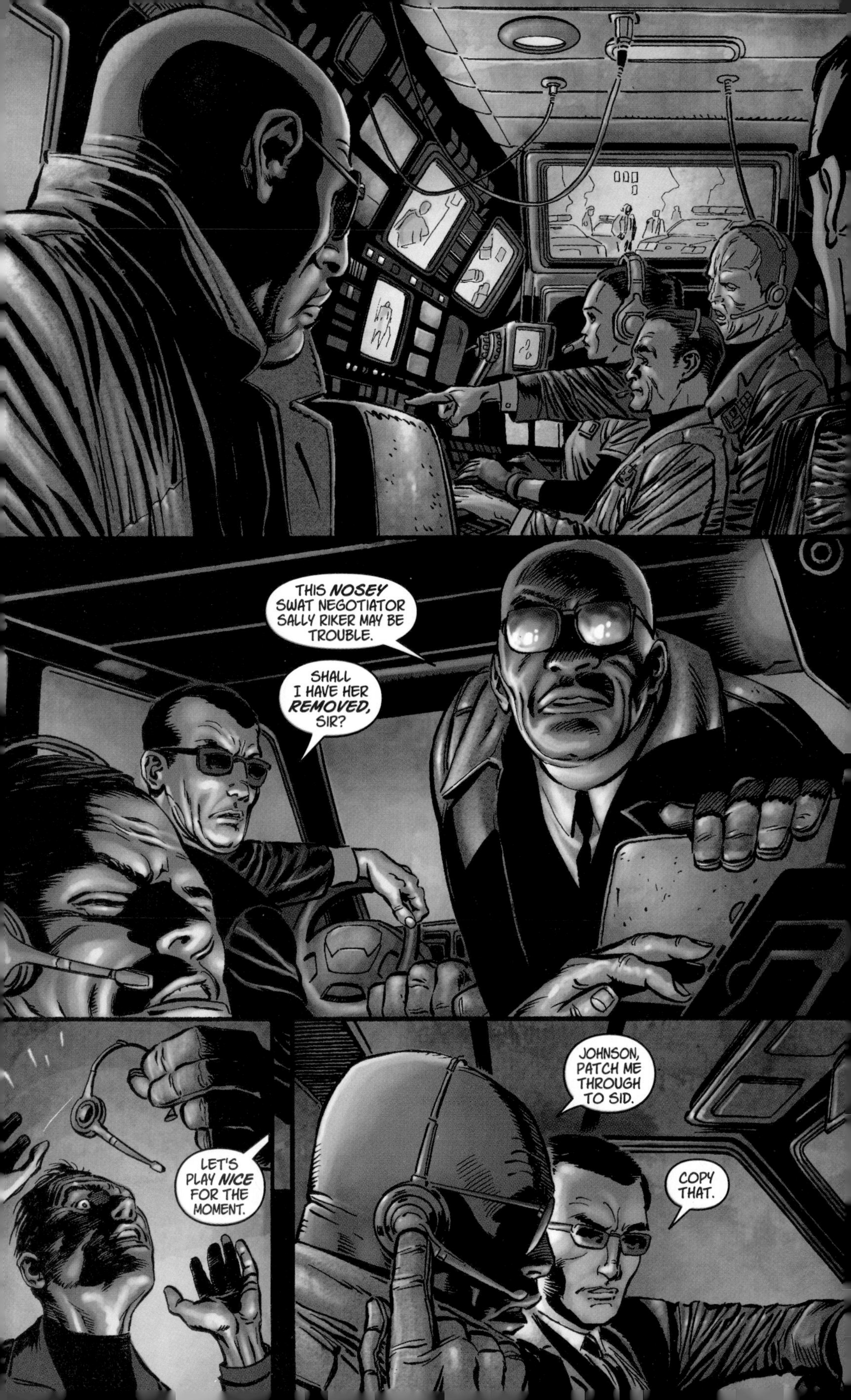
THIS NOSEY SWAT NEGOTIATOR SALLY RIKER MAY BE TROUBLE.
SHALL I HAVE HER REMOVED, SIR?
LET'S PLAY NICE FOR THE MOMENT.
JOHNSON, PATCH ME THROUGH TO SID.
COPY THAT.

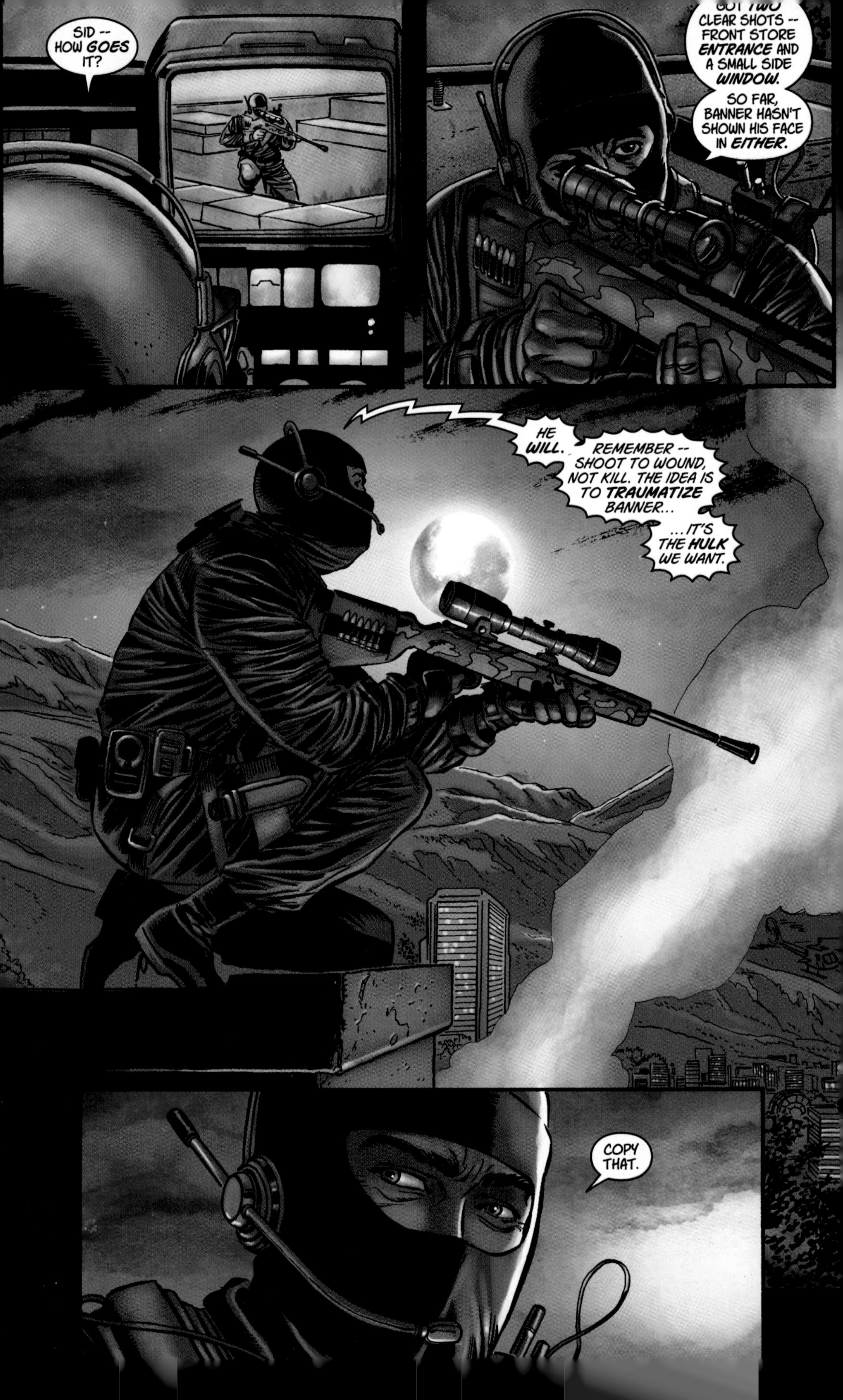
SID -- HOW GOES IT?
GOT TWO CLEAR SHOTS -- FRONT STORE ENTRANCE AND A SMALL SIDE WINDOW.
SO FAR, BANNER HASN'T SHOWN HIS FACE IN EITHER.
HE WILL.
REMEMBER -- SHOOT TO WOUND, NOT KILL. THE IDEA IS TO TRAUMATIZE BANNER...
...IT'S THE HULK WE WANT.
COPY THAT.

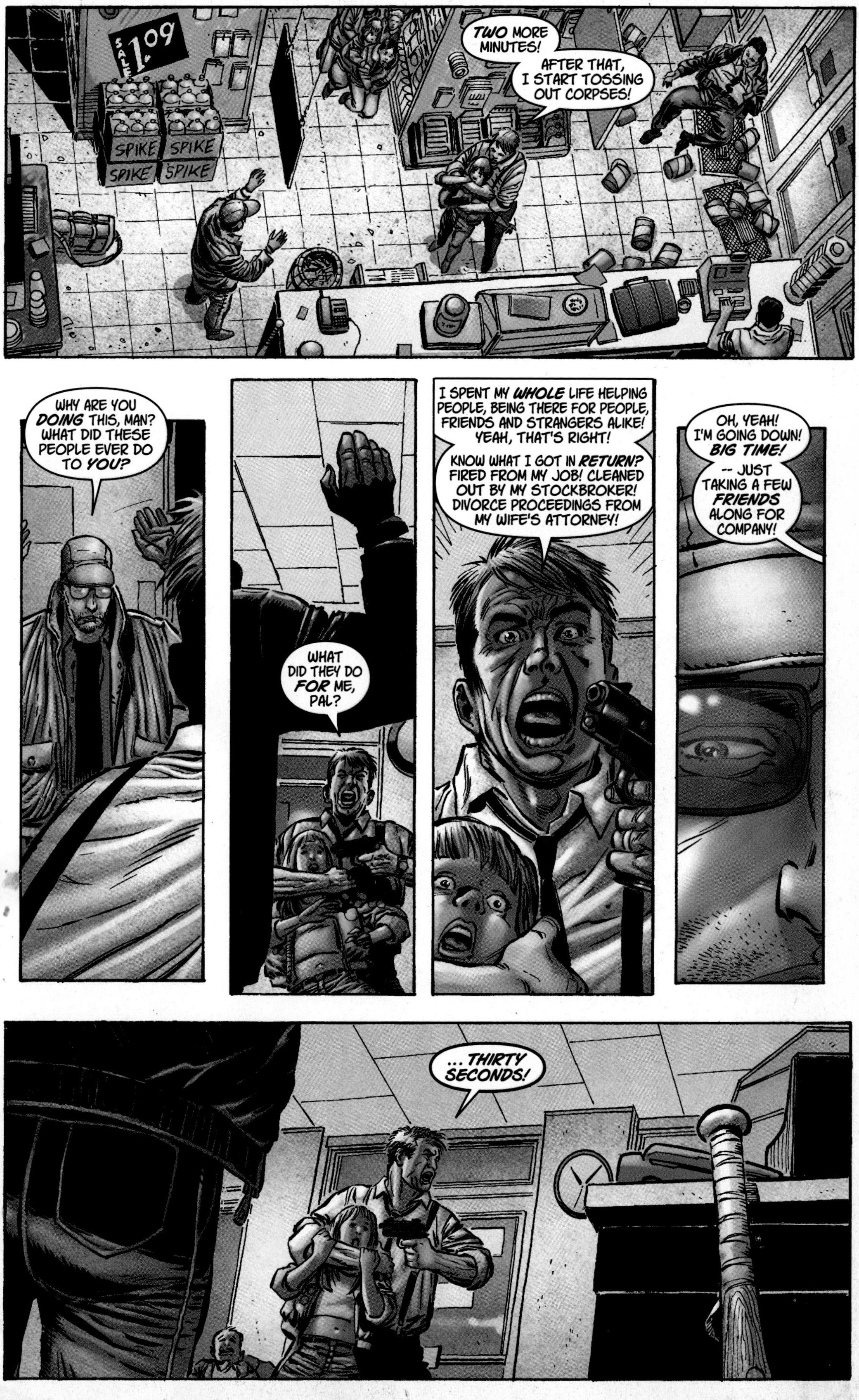
SALE $1.09
SPIKE SPIKE SPIKE SPIKE
TWO MORE MINUTES!
AFTER THAT, I START TOSSING OUT CORPSES!
WHY ARE YOU DOING THIS, MAN? WHAT DID THESE PEOPLE EVER DO TO YOU?
WHAT DID THEY DO FOR ME, PAL?
I SPENT MY WHOLE LIFE HELPING PEOPLE, BEING THERE FOR PEOPLE, FRIENDS AND STRANGERS ALIKE! YEAH, THAT'S RIGHT!
KNOW WHAT I GOT IN RETURN? FIRED FROM MY JOB! CLEANED OUT BY MY STOCKBROKER! DIVORCE PROCEEDINGS FROM MY WIFE'S ATTORNEY!
OH, YEAH! I'M GOING DOWN! BIG TIME!
-- JUST TAKING A FEW FRIENDS ALONG FOR COMPANY!
...THIRTY SECONDS!

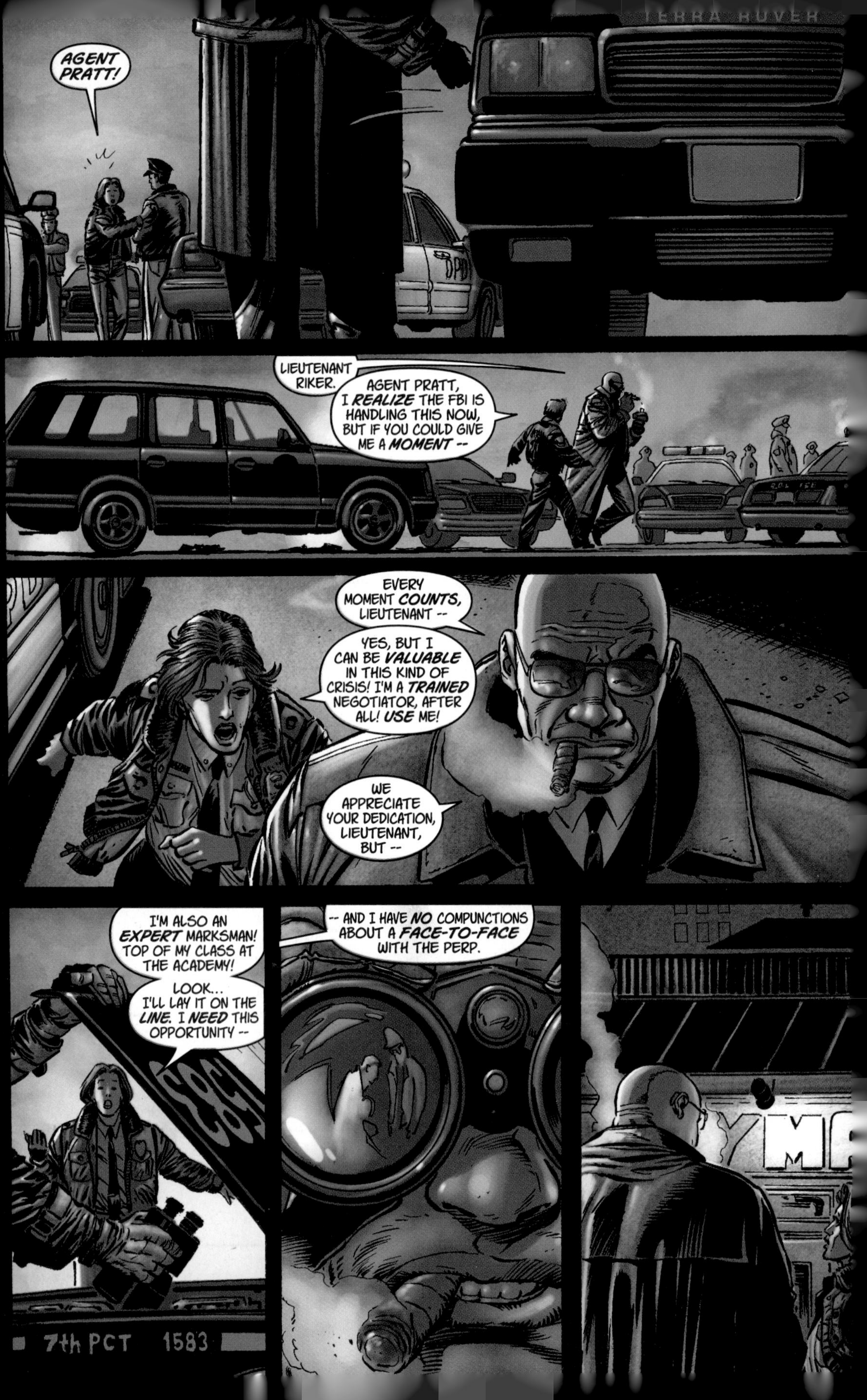
AGENT PRATT!
LIEUTENANT RIKER.
AGENT PRATT, I REALIZE THE FBI IS HANDLING THIS NOW, BUT IF YOU COULD GIVE ME A MOMENT --
EVERY MOMENT COUNTS, LIEUTENANT --
YES, BUT I CAN BE VALUABLE IN THIS KIND OF CRISIS! I'M A TRAINED NEGOTIATOR, AFTER ALL! USE ME!
WE APPRECIATE YOUR DEDICATION, LIEUTENANT, BUT --
I'M ALSO AN EXPERT MARKSMAN! TOP OF MY CLASS AT THE ACADEMY!
LOOK... I'LL LAY IT ON THE LINE. I NEED THIS OPPORTUNITY --
7th PCT 1583
-- AND I HAVE NO COMPUNCTIONS ABOUT A FACE-TO-FACE WITH THE PERP.

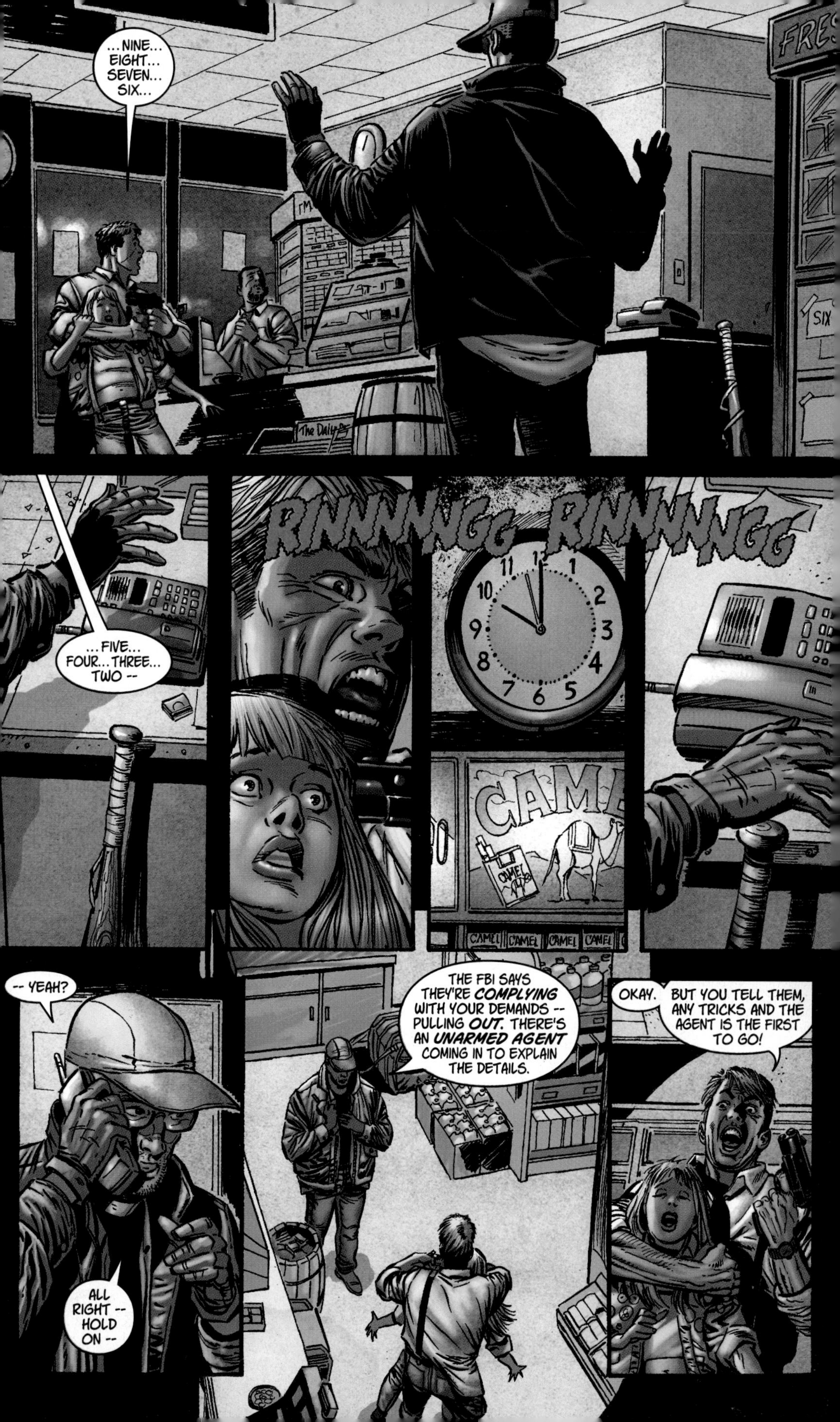
...NINE... EIGHT... SEVEN... SIX...
...FIVE... FOUR...THREE... TWO --
RINNNNNGG RINNNNNGG
-- YEAH?
ALL RIGHT -- HOLD ON --
THE FBI SAYS THEY'RE COMPLYING WITH YOUR DEMANDS -- PULLING OUT. THERE'S AN UNARMED AGENT COMING IN TO EXPLAIN THE DETAILS.
OKAY.
BUT YOU TELL THEM, ANY TRICKS AND THE AGENT IS THE FIRST TO GO!

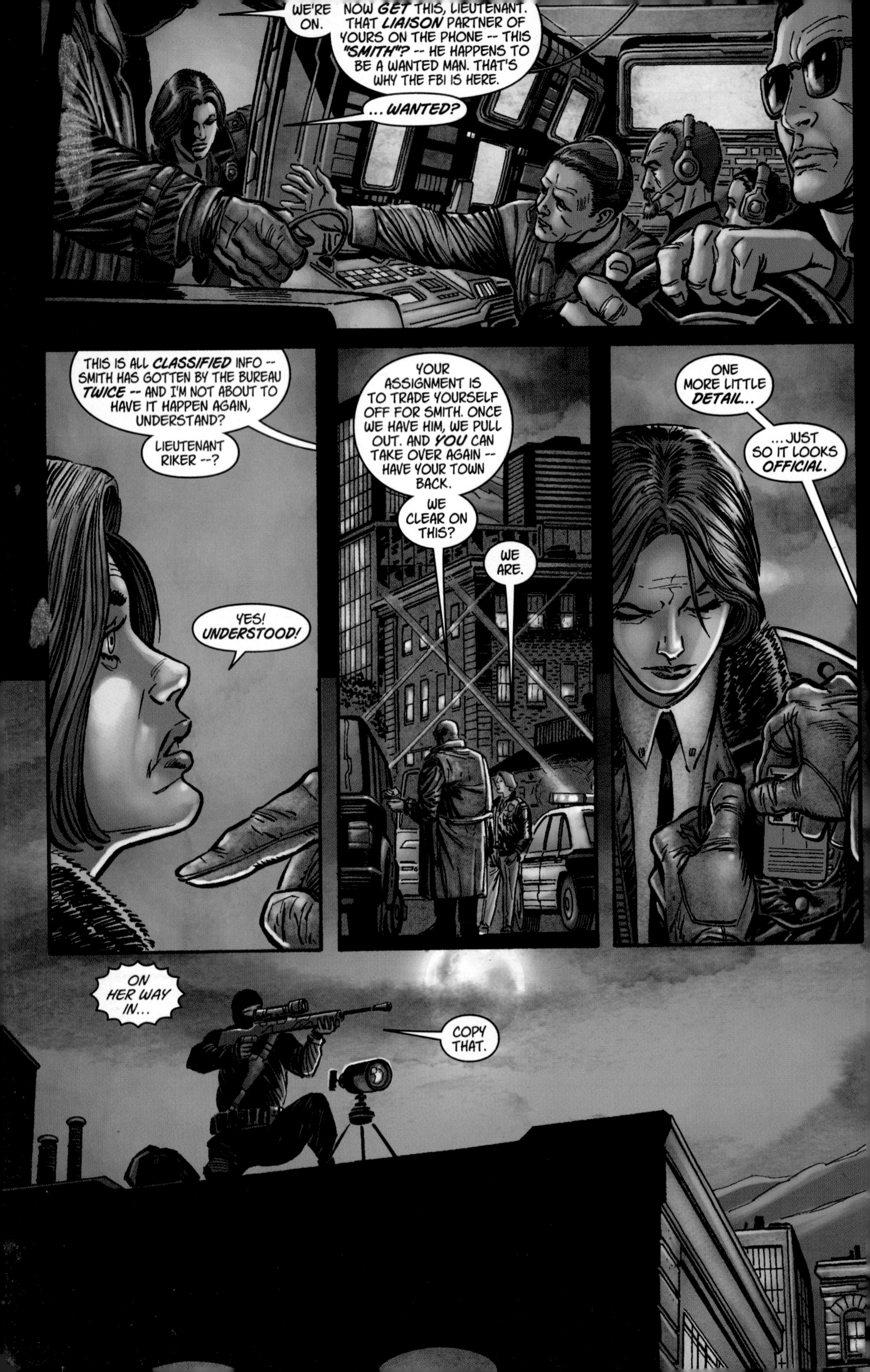

WE'RE ON.
NOW GET THIS, LIEUTENANT. THAT LIAISON PARTNER OF YOURS ON THE PHONE -- THIS "SMITH"? -- HE HAPPENS TO BE A WANTED MAN. THAT'S WHY THE FBI IS HERE.
...WANTED?
THIS IS ALL CLASSIFIED INFO -- SMITH HAS GOTTEN BY THE BUREAU TWICE -- AND I'M NOT ABOUT TO HAVE IT HAPPEN AGAIN, UNDERSTAND?
LIEUTENANT RIKER --?
YES! UNDERSTOOD!
YOUR ASSIGNMENT IS TO TRADE YOURSELF OFF FOR SMITH. ONCE WE HAVE HIM, WE PULL OUT. AND YOU CAN TAKE OVER AGAIN -- HAVE YOUR TOWN BACK.
WE CLEAR ON THIS?
WE ARE.
ONE MORE LITTLE DETAIL...
...JUST SO IT LOOKS OFFICIAL.
ON HER WAY IN...
COPY THAT.

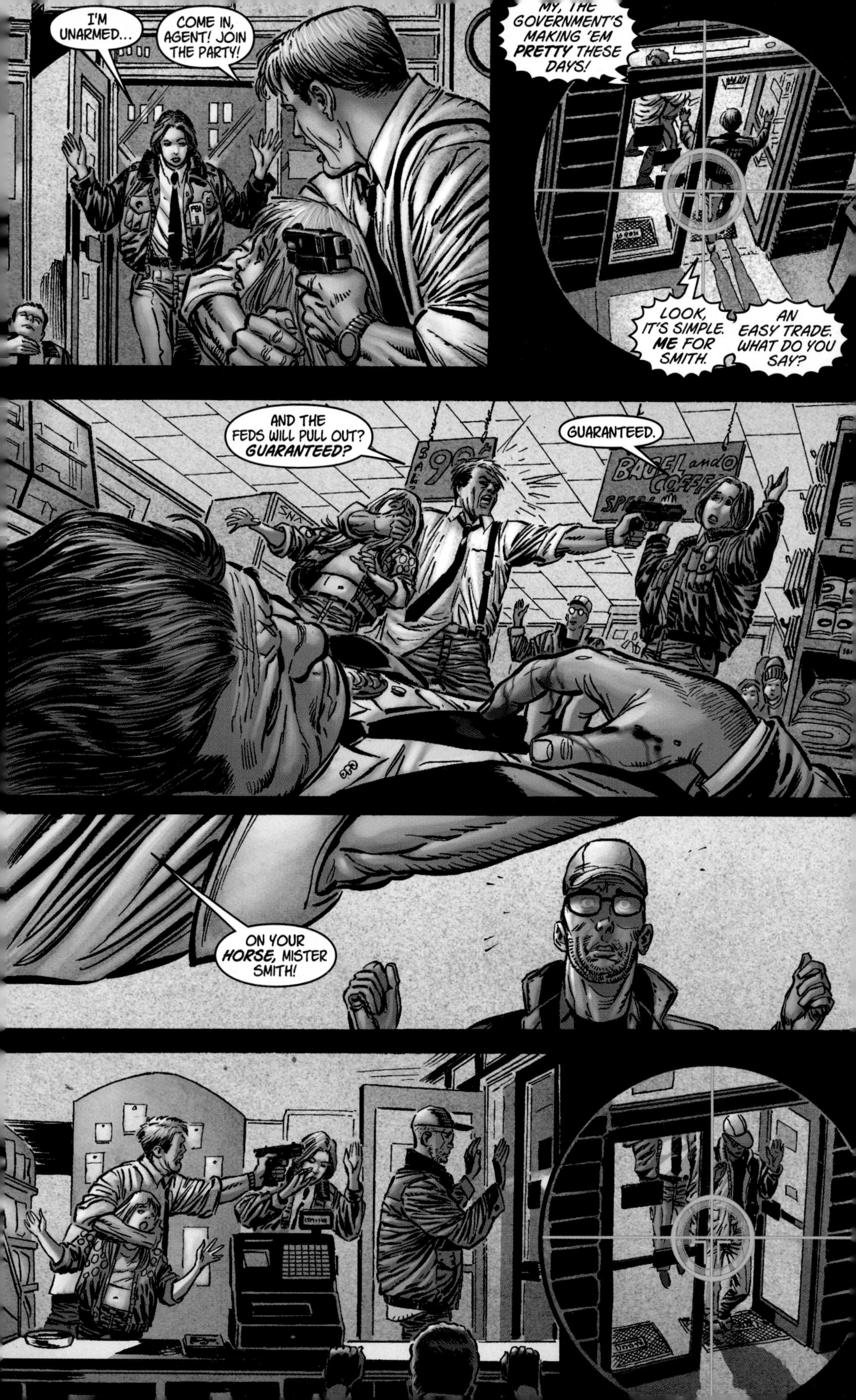

I'M UNARMED...
COME IN, AGENT! JOIN THE PARTY!
MY, THE GOVERNMENT'S MAKING 'EM PRETTY THESE DAYS!
LOOK, IT'S SIMPLE. ME FOR SMITH.
AN EASY TRADE. WHAT DO YOU SAY?
AND THE FEDS WILL PULL OUT? GUARANTEED?
GUARANTEED.
BAGEL and COFFEE
ON YOUR HORSE, MISTER SMITH!

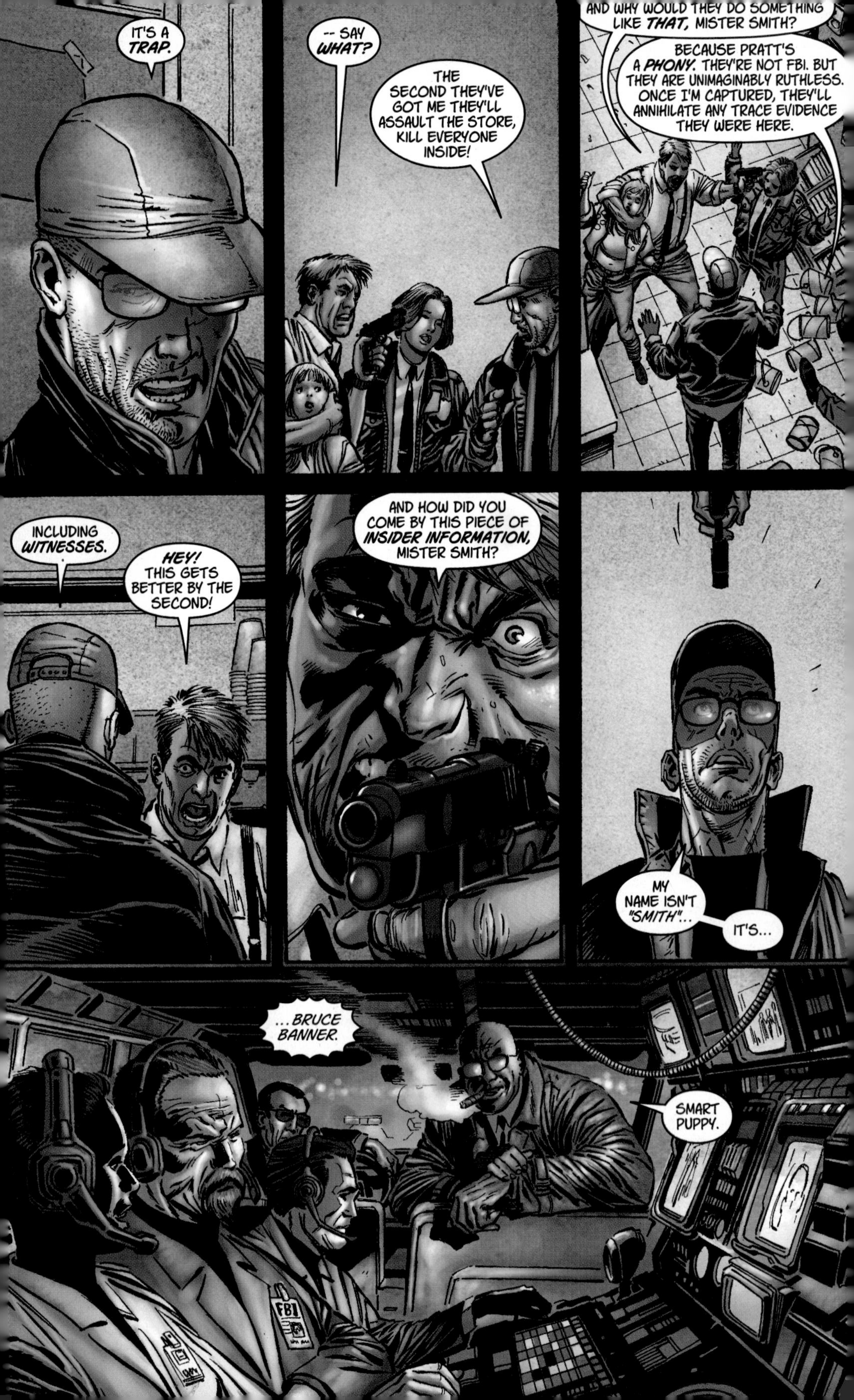
IT'S A TRAP.
-- SAY WHAT?
THE SECOND THEY'VE GOT ME THEY'LL ASSAULT THE STORE, KILL EVERYONE INSIDE!
AND WHY WOULD THEY DO SOMETHING LIKE THAT, MISTER SMITH?
BECAUSE PRATT'S A PHONY. THEY'RE NOT FBI. BUT THEY ARE UNIMAGINABLY RUTHLESS. ONCE I'M CAPTURED, THEY'LL ANNIHILATE ANY TRACE EVIDENCE THEY WERE HERE.
INCLUDING WITNESSES.
HEY! THIS GETS BETTER BY THE SECOND!
AND HOW DID YOU COME BY THIS PIECE OF INSIDER INFORMATION, MISTER SMITH?
MY NAME ISN'T "SMITH"...
IT'S...
...BRUCE BANNER.
SMART PUPPY.
FBI

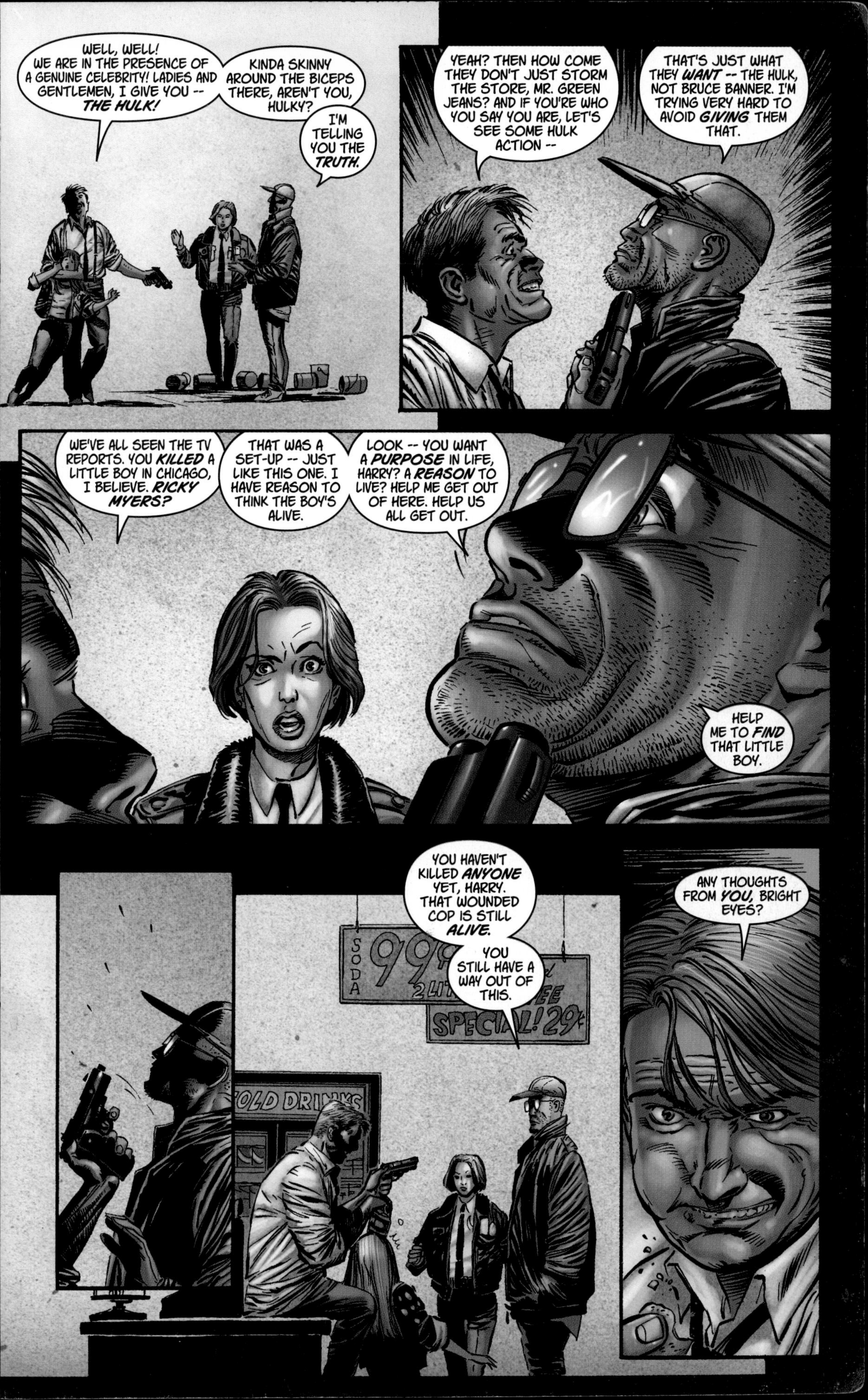
WELL, WELL! WE ARE IN THE PRESENCE OF A GENUINE CELEBRITY! LADIES AND GENTLEMEN, I GIVE YOU -- THE HULK!
KINDA SKINNY AROUND THE BICEPS THERE, AREN'T YOU, HULKY?
I'M TELLING YOU THE TRUTH.
YEAH? THEN HOW COME THEY DON'T JUST STORM THE STORE, MR. GREEN JEANS? AND IF YOU'RE WHO YOU SAY YOU ARE, LET'S SEE SOME HULK ACTION --
THAT'S JUST WHAT THEY WANT -- THE HULK, NOT BRUCE BANNER. I'M TRYING VERY HARD TO AVOID GIVING THEM THAT.
WE'VE ALL SEEN THE TV REPORTS. YOU KILLED A LITTLE BOY IN CHICAGO, I BELIEVE. RICKY MYERS?
THAT WAS A SET-UP -- JUST LIKE THIS ONE. I HAVE REASON TO THINK THE BOY'S ALIVE.
LOOK -- YOU WANT A PURPOSE IN LIFE, HARRY? A REASON TO LIVE? HELP ME GET OUT OF HERE. HELP US ALL GET OUT.
HELP ME TO FIND THAT LITTLE BOY.
YOU HAVEN'T KILLED ANYONE YET, HARRY. THAT WOUNDED COP IS STILL ALIVE.
YOU STILL HAVE A WAY OUT OF THIS.
SODA
SPECIAL! 29¢
COLD DRINKS
ANY THOUGHTS FROM YOU, BRIGHT EYES?

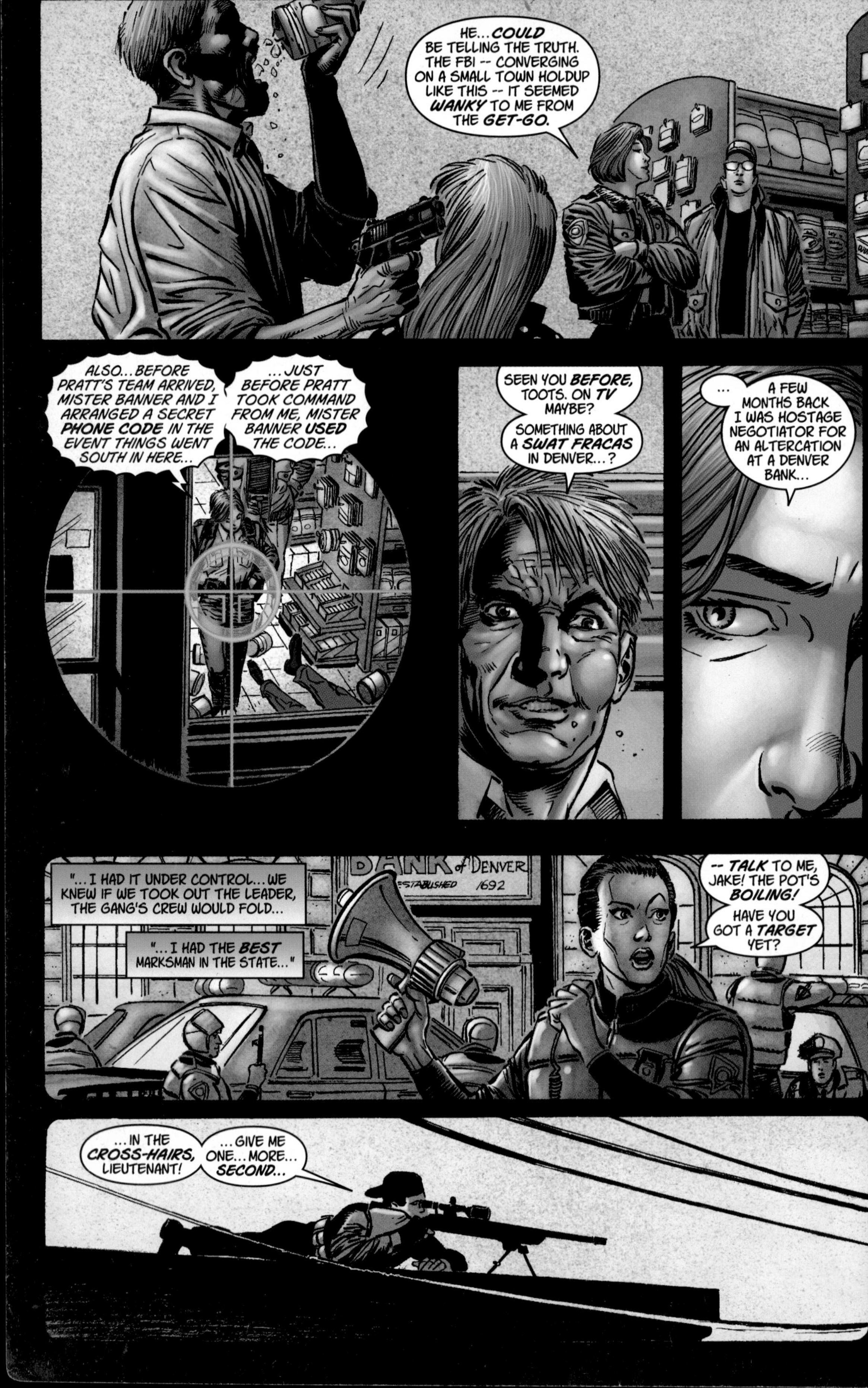
HE...COULD BE TELLING THE TRUTH. THE FBI -- CONVERGING ON A SMALL TOWN HOLDUP LIKE THIS -- IT SEEMED WANKY TO ME FROM THE GET-GO.
ALSO...BEFORE PRATT'S TEAM ARRIVED, MISTER BANNER AND I ARRANGED A SECRET PHONE CODE IN THE EVENT THINGS WENT SOUTH IN HERE...
...JUST BEFORE PRATT TOOK COMMAND FROM ME, MISTER BANNER USED THE CODE...
SEEN YOU BEFORE, TOOTS. ON TV MAYBE?
SOMETHING ABOUT A SWAT FRACAS IN DENVER...?
... A FEW MONTHS BACK I WAS HOSTAGE NEGOTIATOR FOR AN ALTERCATION AT A DENVER BANK...
BANK of DENVER
ESTABLISHED 1692
"...I HAD IT UNDER CONTROL...WE KNEW IF WE TOOK OUT THE LEADER, THE GANG'S CREW WOULD FOLD...
"...I HAD THE BEST MARKSMAN IN THE STATE..."
-- TALK TO ME, JAKE! THE POT'S BOILING!
HAVE YOU GOT A TARGET YET?
...IN THE CROSS-HAIRS, LIEUTENANT!
...GIVE ME ONE...MORE... SECOND...

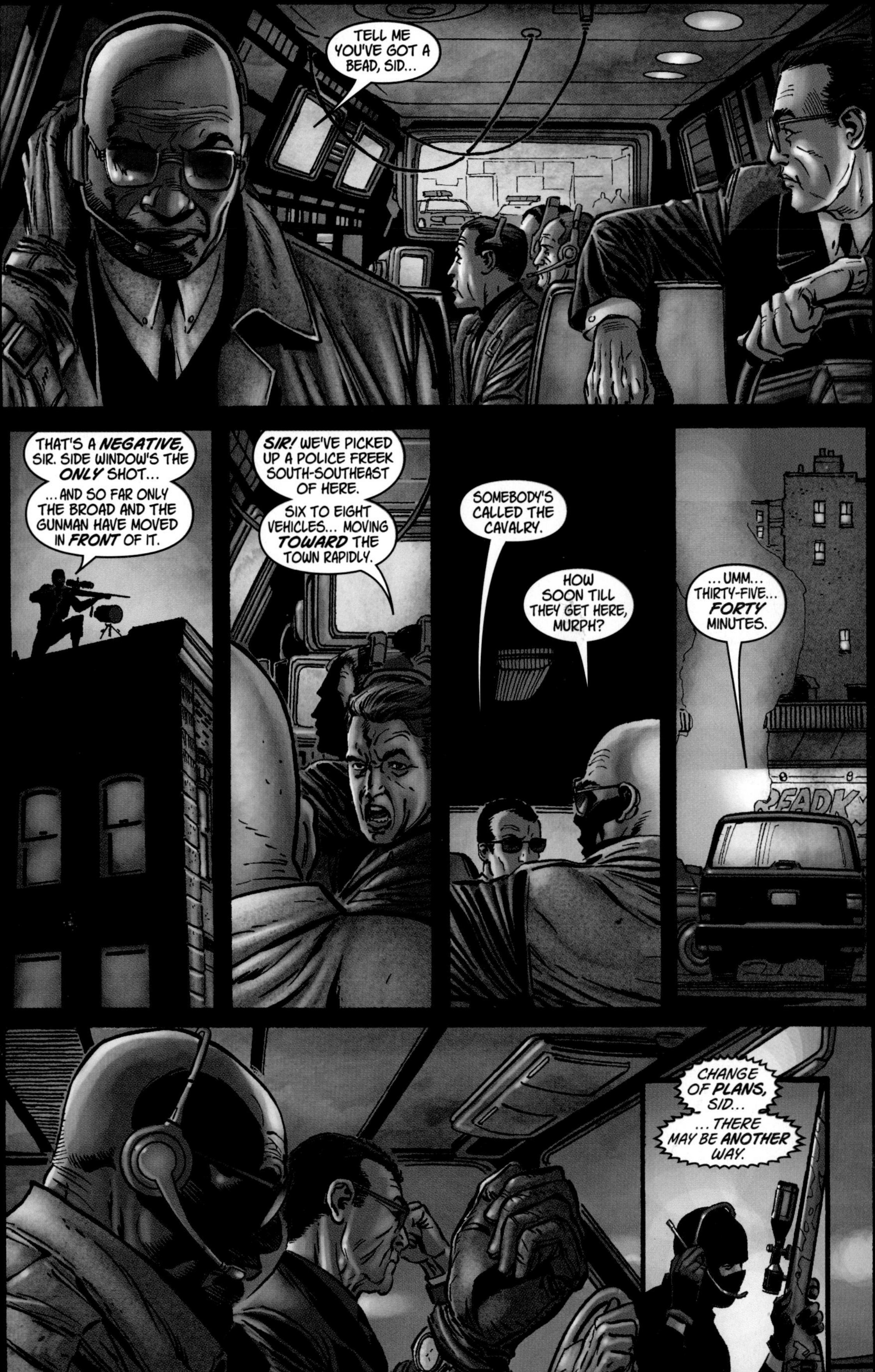

TELL ME YOU'VE GOT A BEAD, SID...
THAT'S A NEGATIVE, SIR. SIDE WINDOW'S THE ONLY SHOT...
...AND SO FAR ONLY THE BROAD AND THE GUNMAN HAVE MOVED IN FRONT OF IT.
SIR! WE'VE PICKED UP A POLICE FREEK SOUTH-SOUTHEAST OF HERE.
SIX TO EIGHT VEHICLES... MOVING TOWARD THE TOWN RAPIDLY.
SOMEBODY'S CALLED THE CAVALRY.
HOW SOON TILL THEY GET HERE, MURPH?
...UMM... THIRTY-FIVE... FORTY MINUTES.
CHANGE OF PLANS, SID...
...THERE MAY BE ANOTHER WAY.

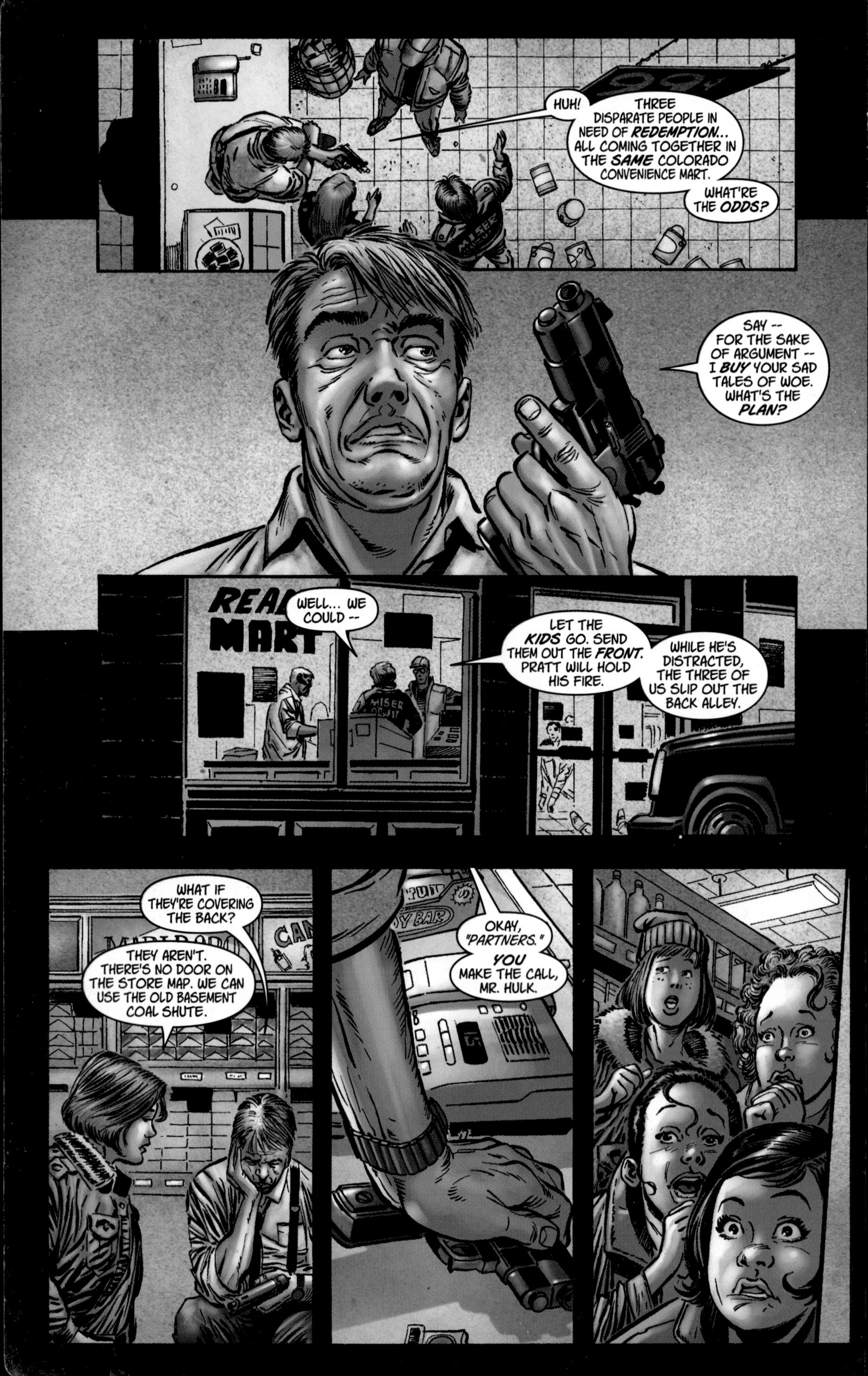
HUH!
THREE DISPARATE PEOPLE IN NEED OF REDEMPTION... ALL COMING TOGETHER IN THE SAME COLORADO CONVENIENCE MART.
WHAT'RE THE ODDS?
SAY -- FOR THE SAKE OF ARGUMENT -- I BUY YOUR SAD TALES OF WOE. WHAT'S THE PLAN?
MART
WELL... WE COULD --
LET THE KIDS GO. SEND THEM OUT THE FRONT. PRATT WILL HOLD HIS FIRE.
WHILE HE'S DISTRACTED, THE THREE OF US SLIP OUT THE BACK ALLEY.
WHAT IF THEY'RE COVERING THE BACK?
THEY AREN'T. THERE'S NO DOOR ON THE STORE MAP. WE CAN USE THE OLD BASEMENT COAL SHUTE.
OKAY, "PARTNERS." YOU MAKE THE CALL, MR. HULK.

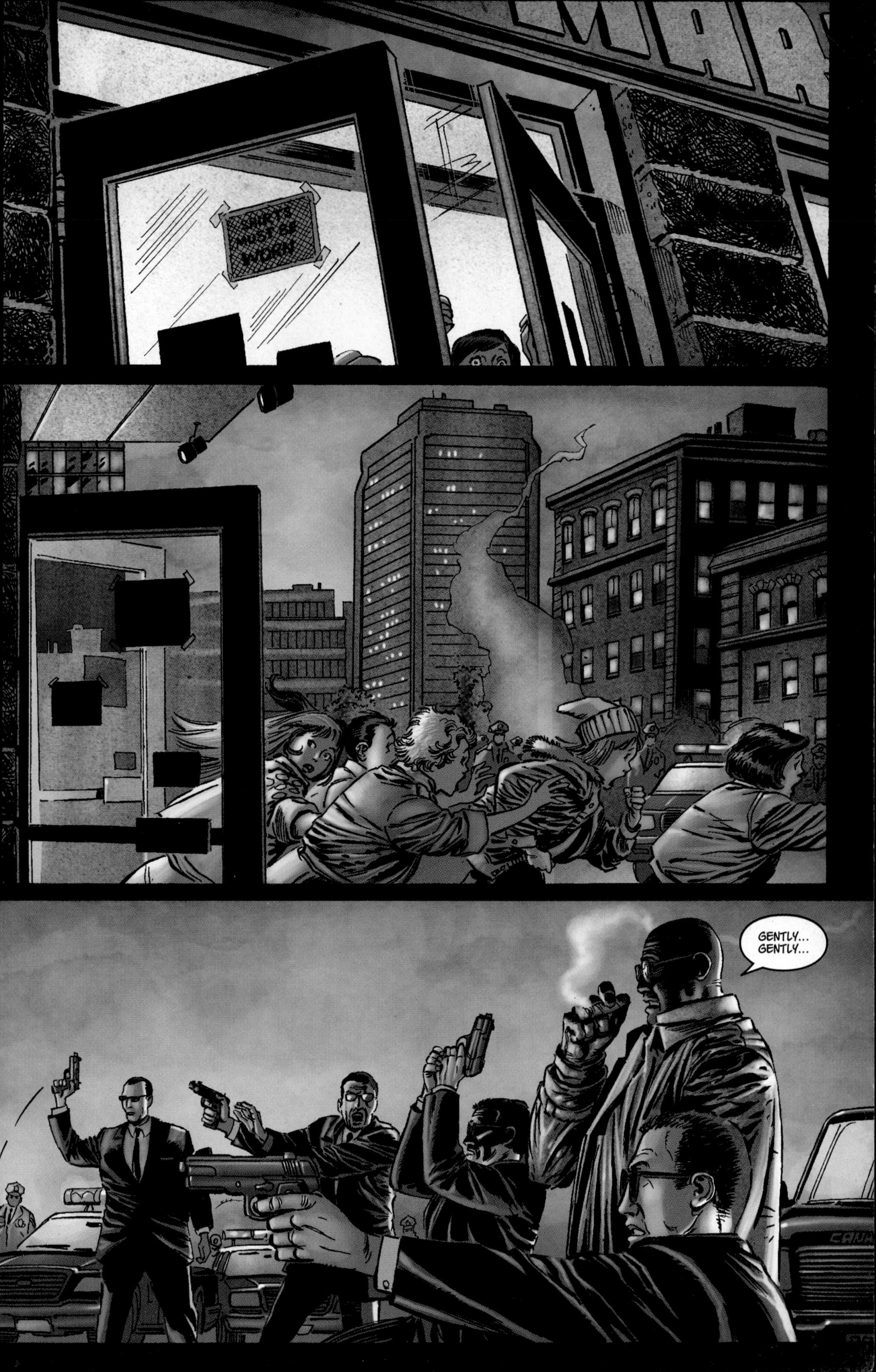
SHIRTS MUST BE WORN
GENTLY... GENTLY...

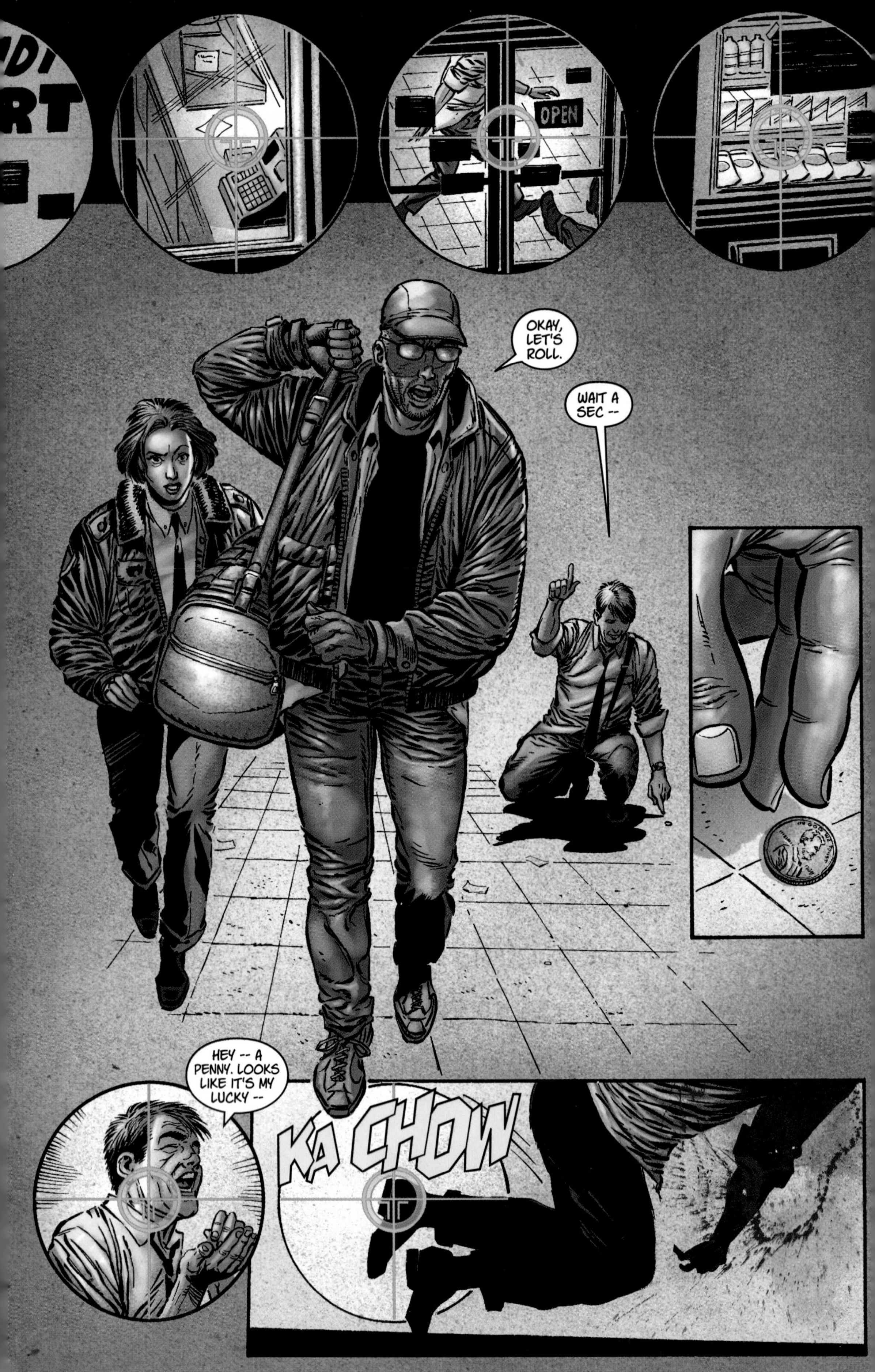
OPEN
OKAY, LET'S ROLL.
WAIT A SEC --
HEY -- A PENNY. LOOKS LIKE IT'S MY LUCKY --
KA CHOW

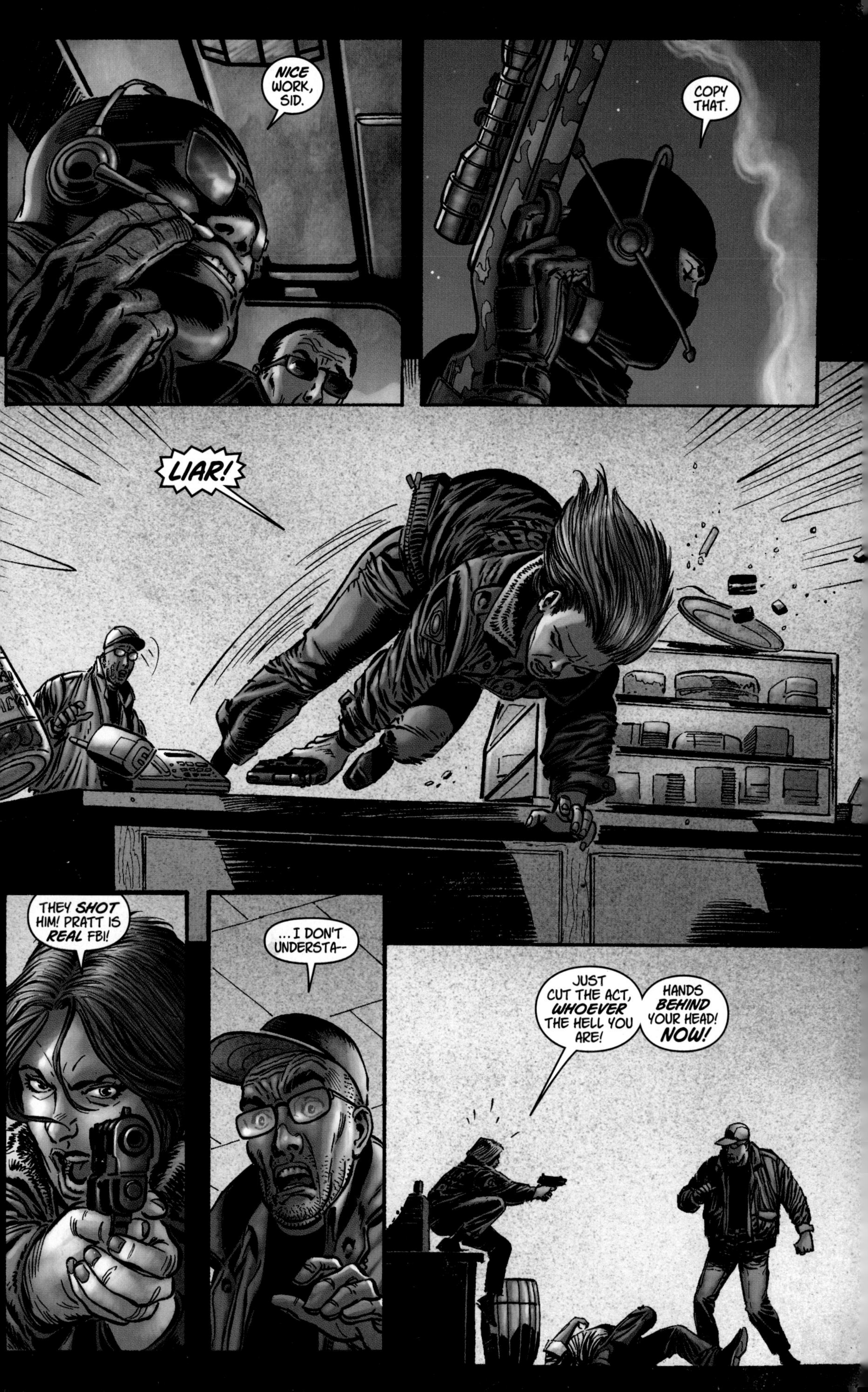

NICE WORK, SID.
COPY THAT.
LIAR!
THEY SHOT HIM! PRATT IS REAL FBI!
...I DON'T UNDERSTA--
JUST CUT THE ACT, WHOEVER THE HELL YOU ARE!
HANDS BEHIND YOUR HEAD! NOW!

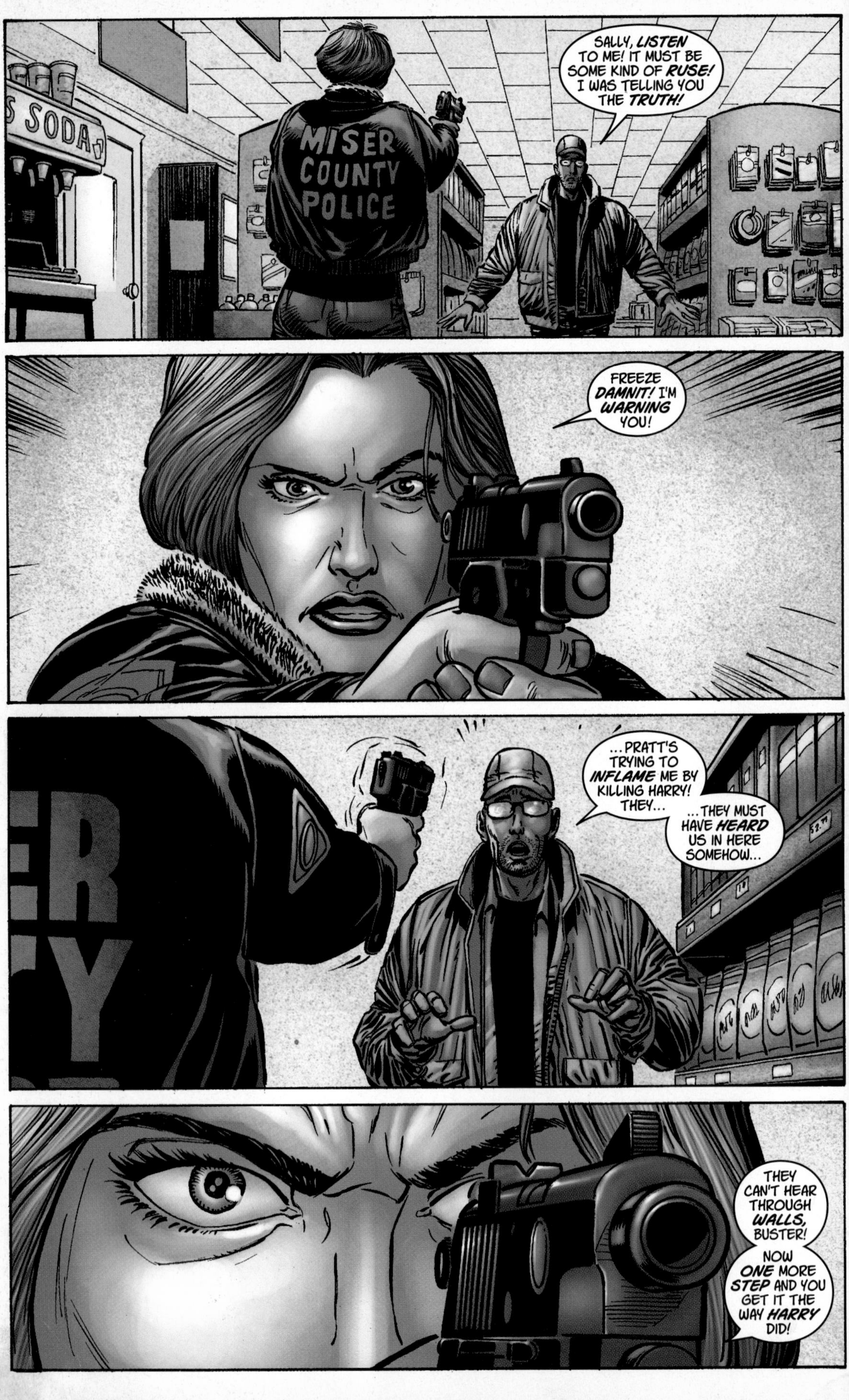
S SODA
MISER COUNTY POLICE
SALLY, LISTEN TO ME! IT MUST BE SOME KIND OF RUSE! I WAS TELLING YOU THE TRUTH!
FREEZE DAMNIT! I'M WARNING YOU!
...PRATT'S TRYING TO INFLAME ME BY KILLING HARRY! THEY...
...THEY MUST HAVE HEARD US IN HERE SOMEHOW...
THEY CAN'T HEAR THROUGH WALLS, BUSTER!
NOW ONE MORE STEP AND YOU GET IT THE WAY HARRY DID!

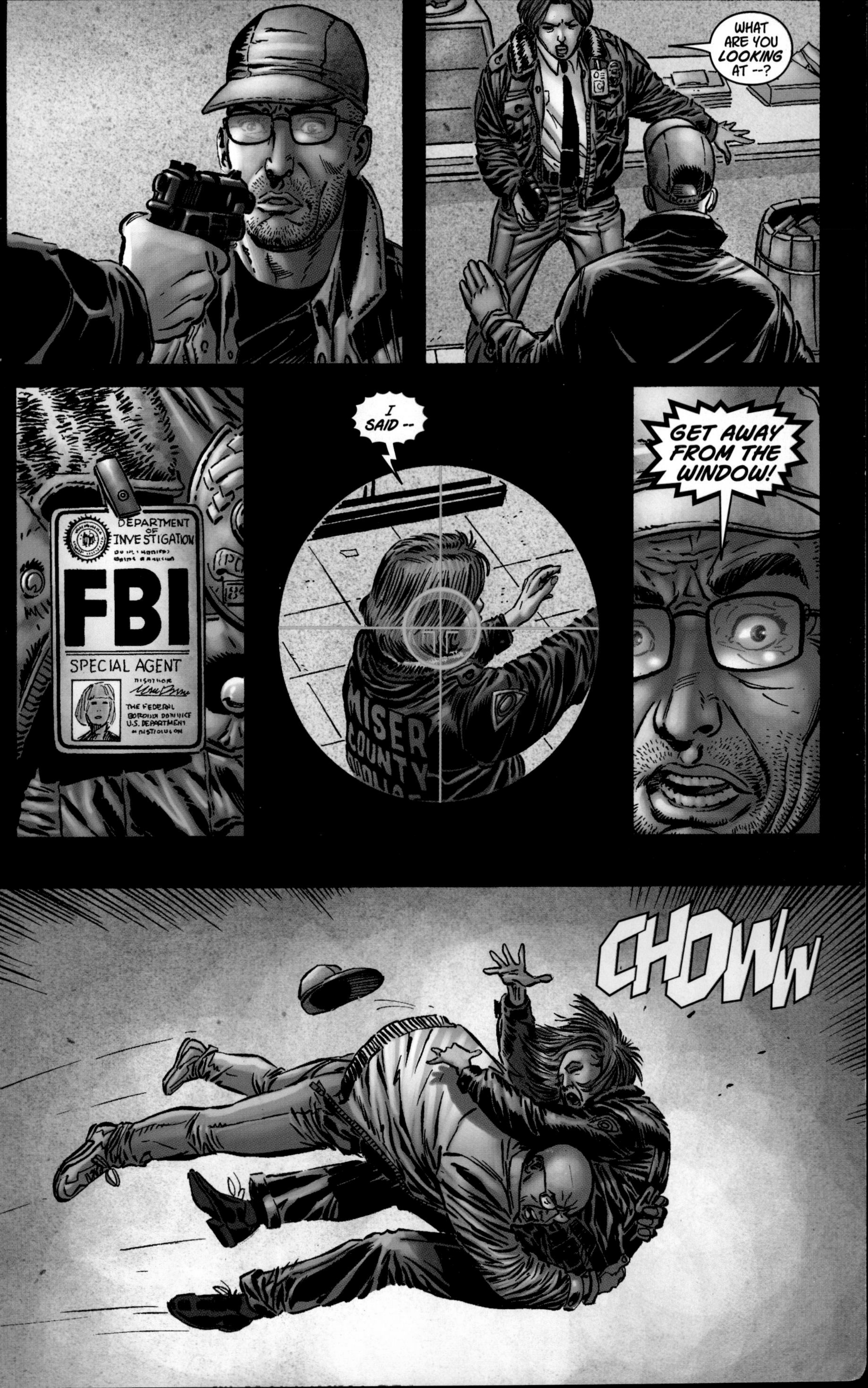
WHAT ARE YOU LOOKING AT --?
DEPARTMENT OF INVESTIGATION
FBI
SPECIAL AGENT
I SAID --
MISER COUNTY
GET AWAY FROM THE WINDOW!
CHOWW

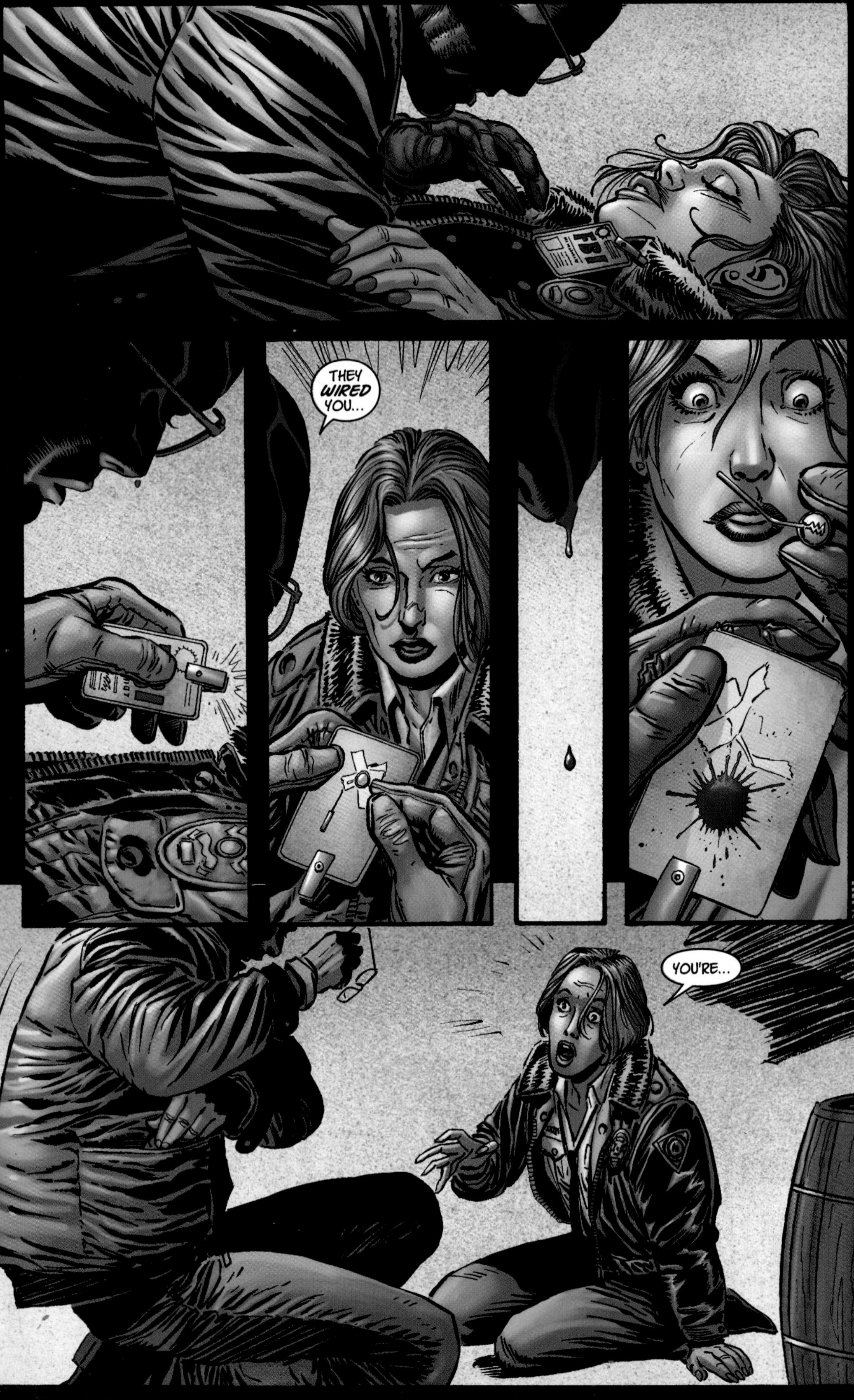
FBI
THEY WIRED YOU...
YOU'RE...

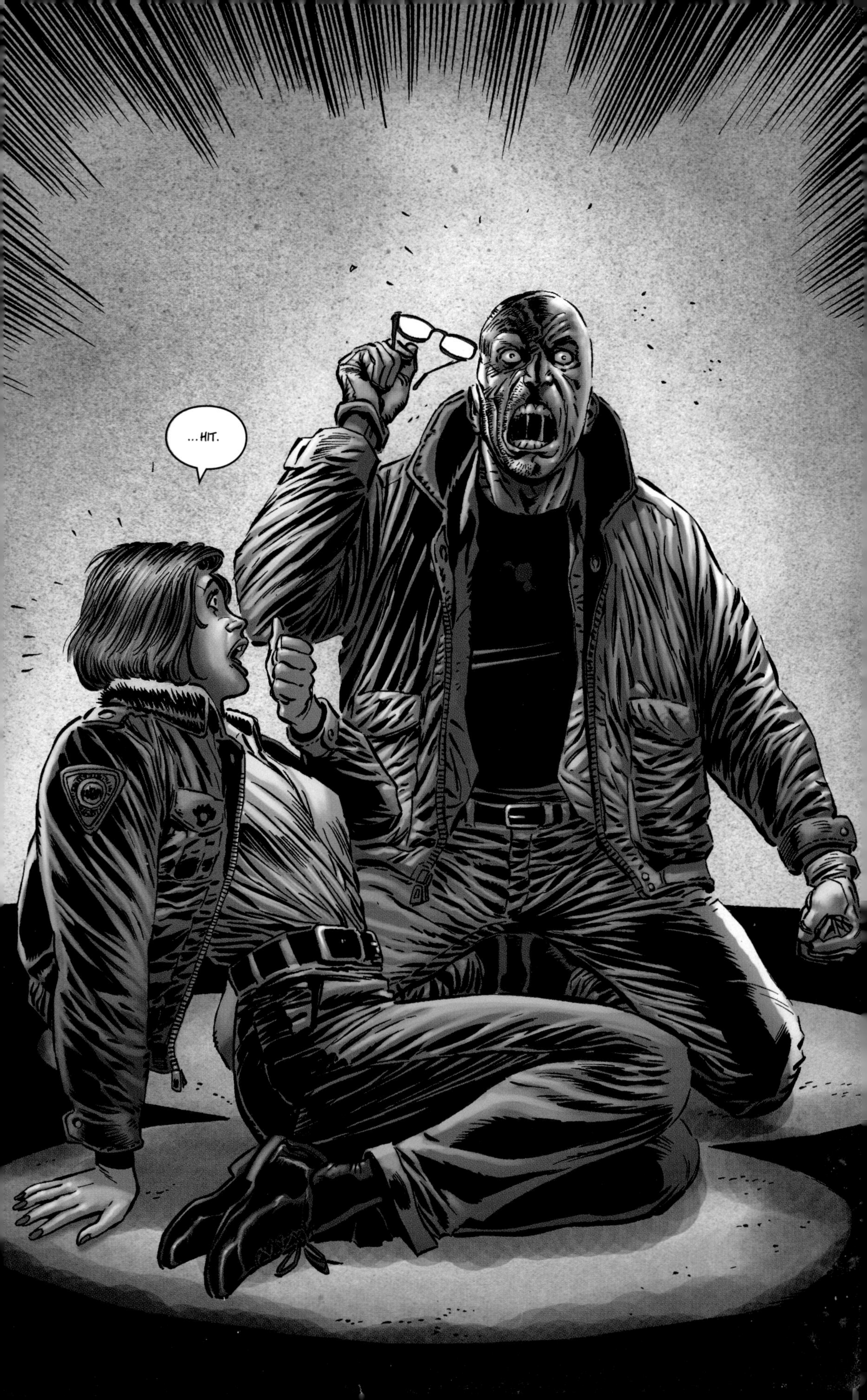
...HIT.

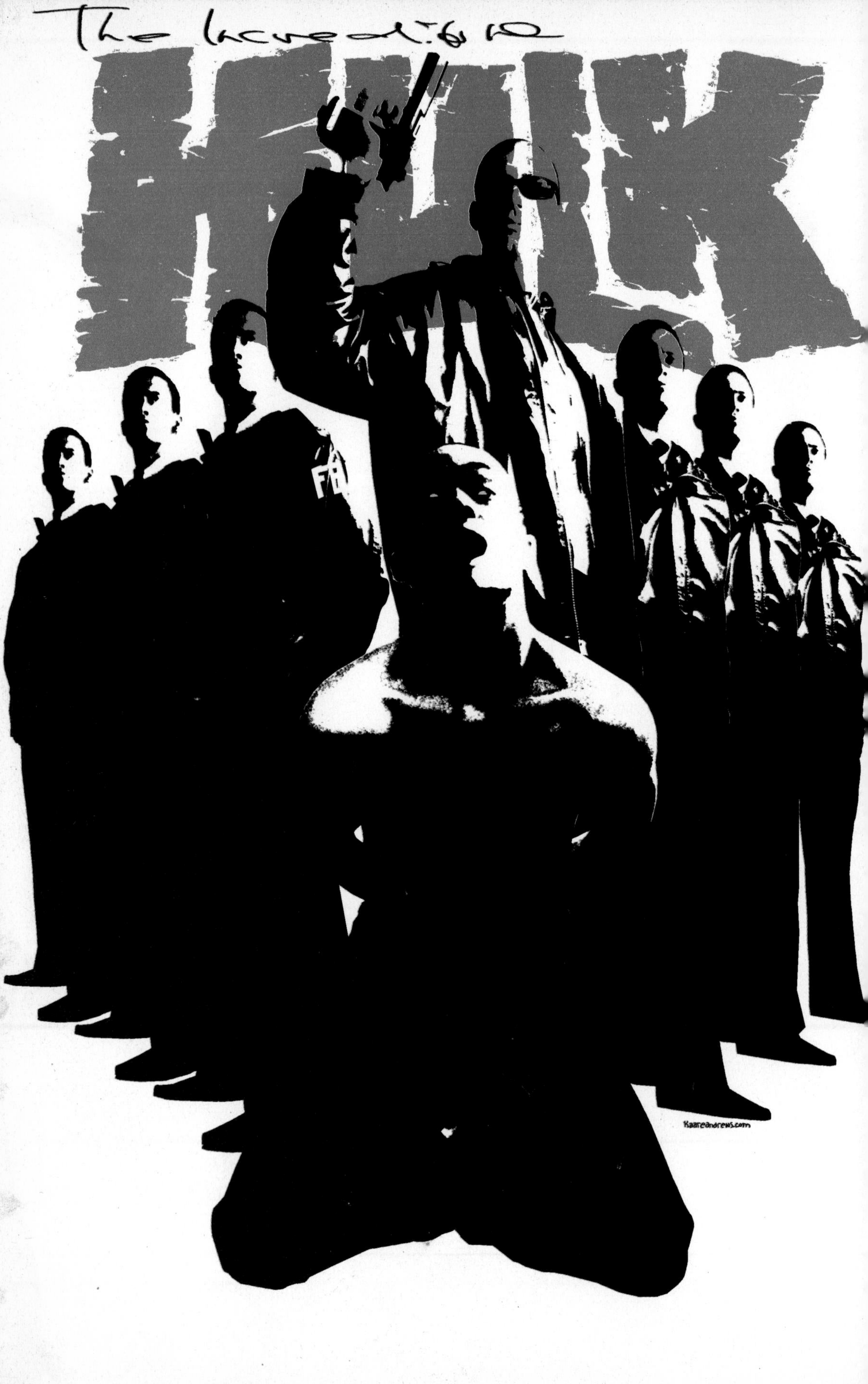
The Incredible
HULK
Kaareandrews.com

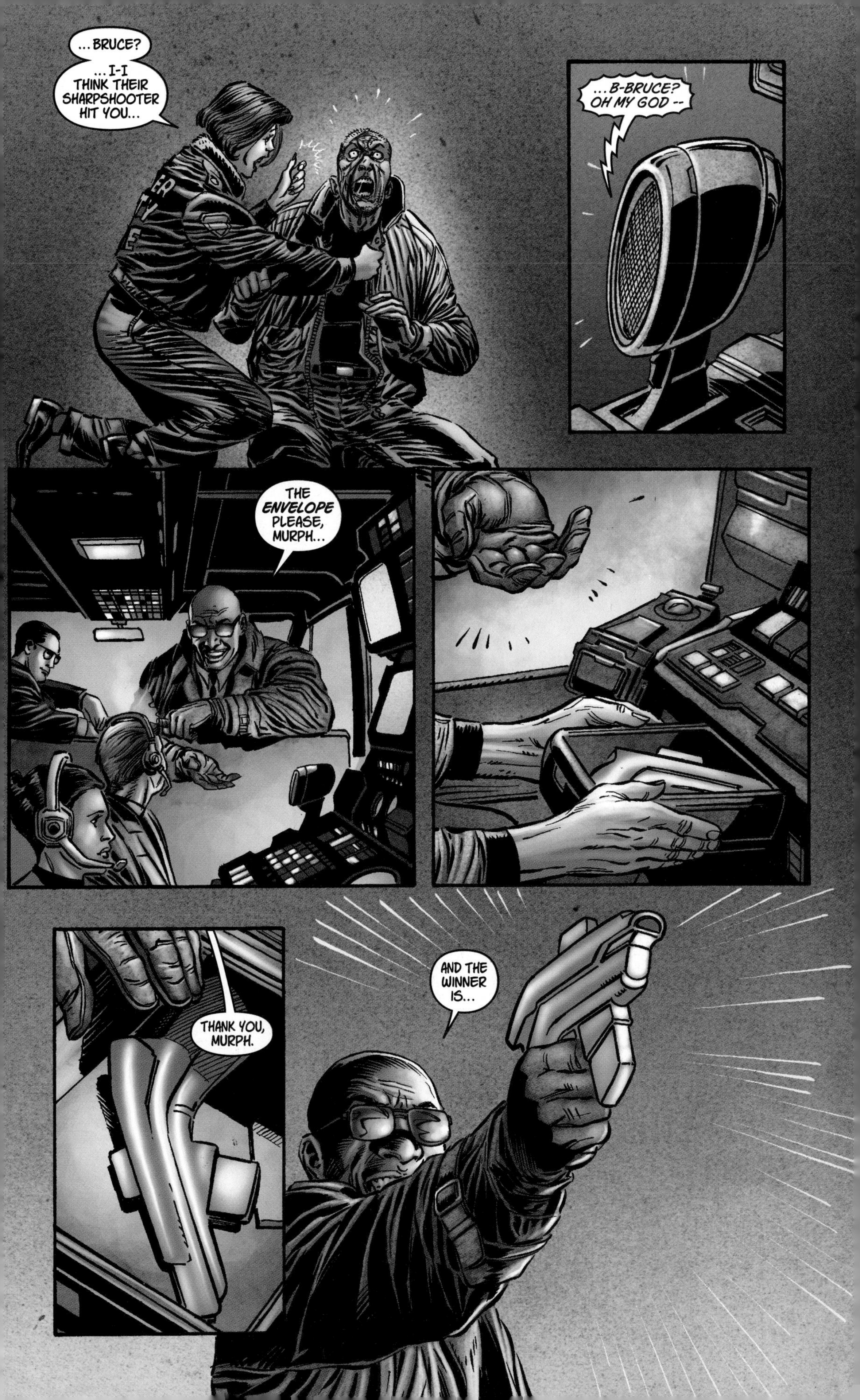
... BRUCE?
... I-I THINK THEIR SHARPSHOOTER HIT YOU...
... B-BRUCE? OH MY GOD --
THE ENVELOPE PLEASE, MURPH...
THANK YOU, MURPH.
AND THE WINNER IS...

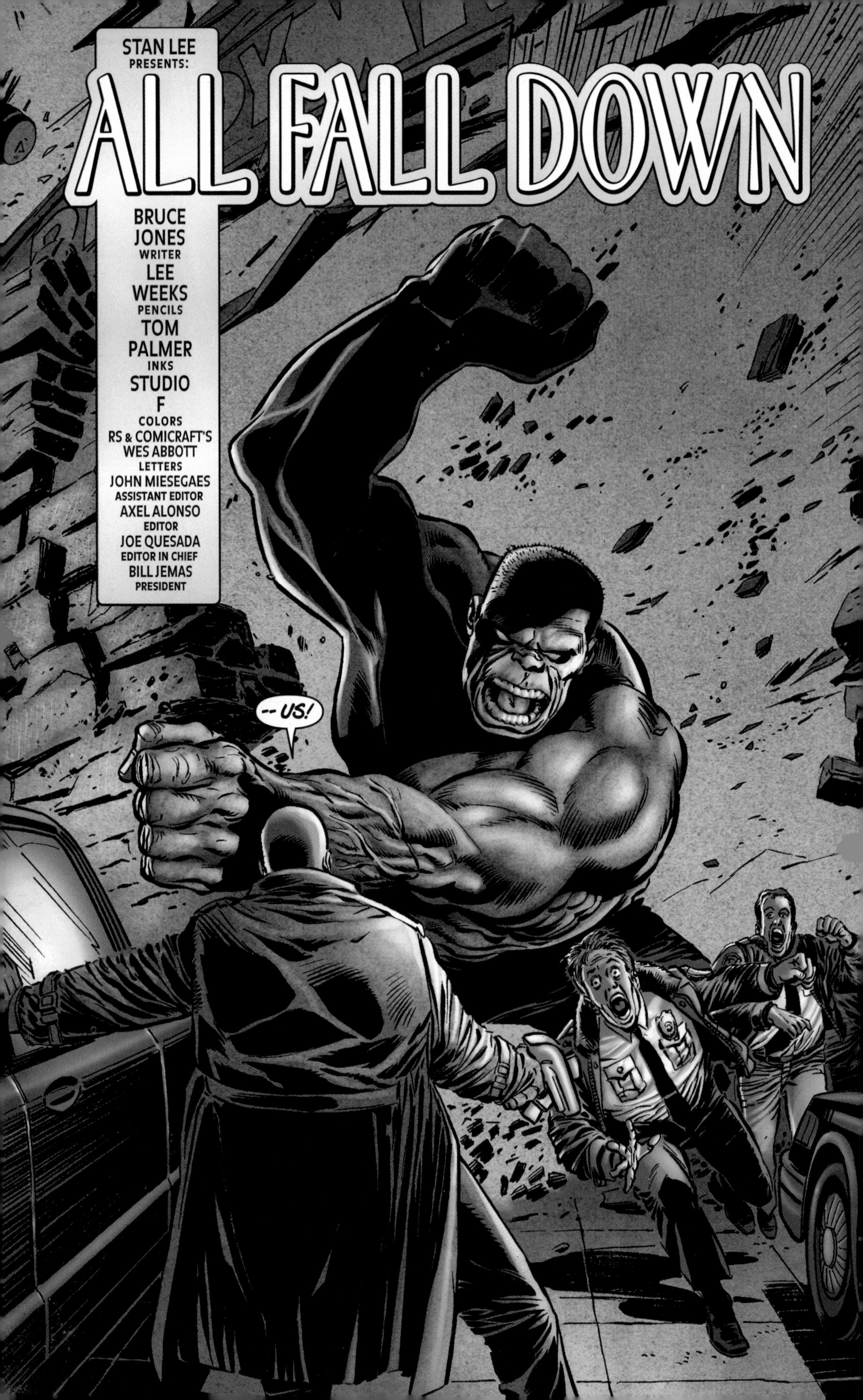
STAN LEE PRESENTS:
ALL FALL DOWN
BRUCE JONES WRITER
LEE WEEKS PENCILS
TOM PALMER INKS
STUDIO F COLORS
RS & COMICRAFT'S WES ABBOTT LETTERS
JOHN MIESEGAES ASSISTANT EDITOR
AXEL ALONSO EDITOR
JOE QUESADA EDITOR IN CHIEF
BILL JEMAS PRESIDENT
--US!

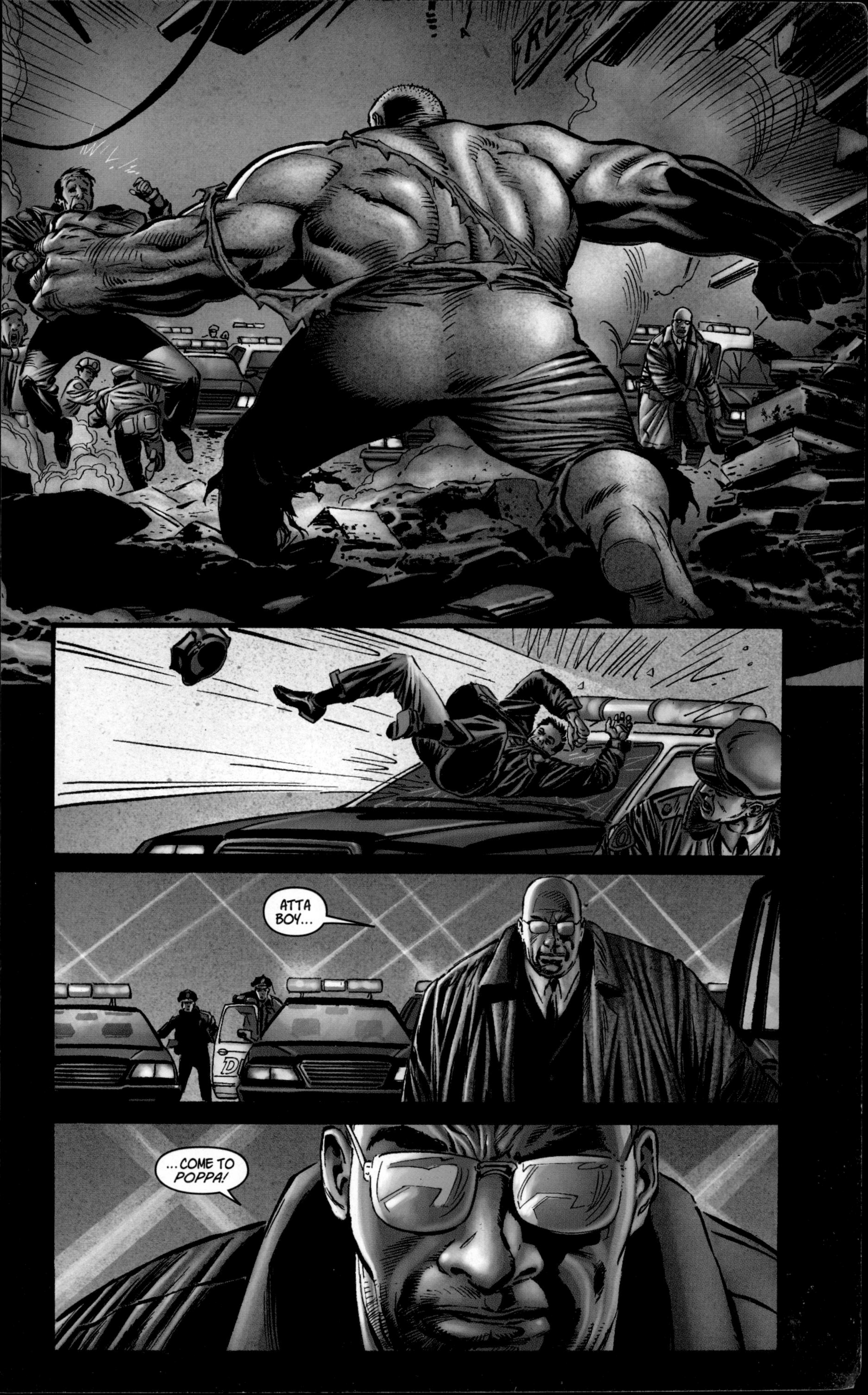
ATTA BOY...
...COME TO POPPA!

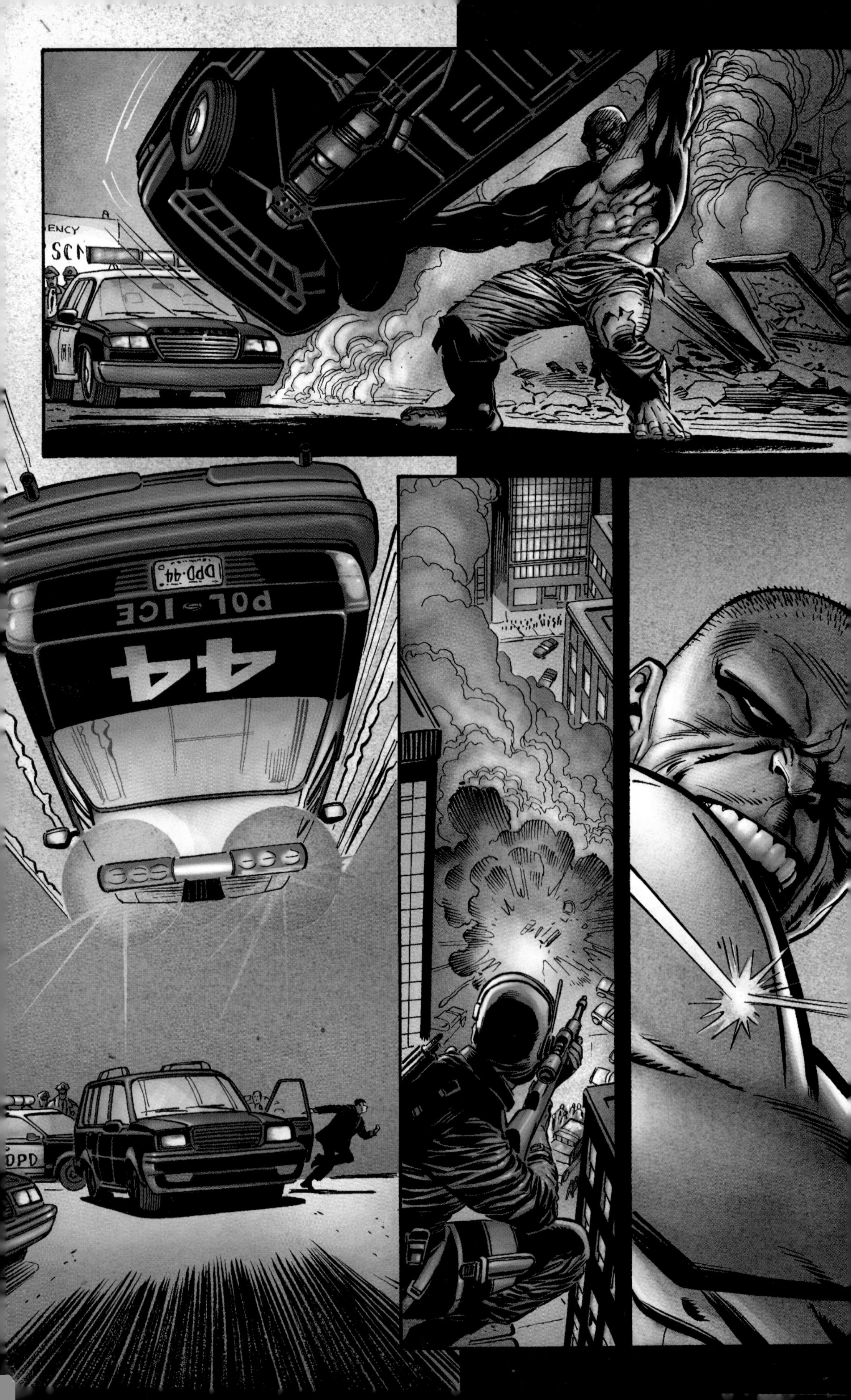
DPD·44
POL ICE
44
DPD

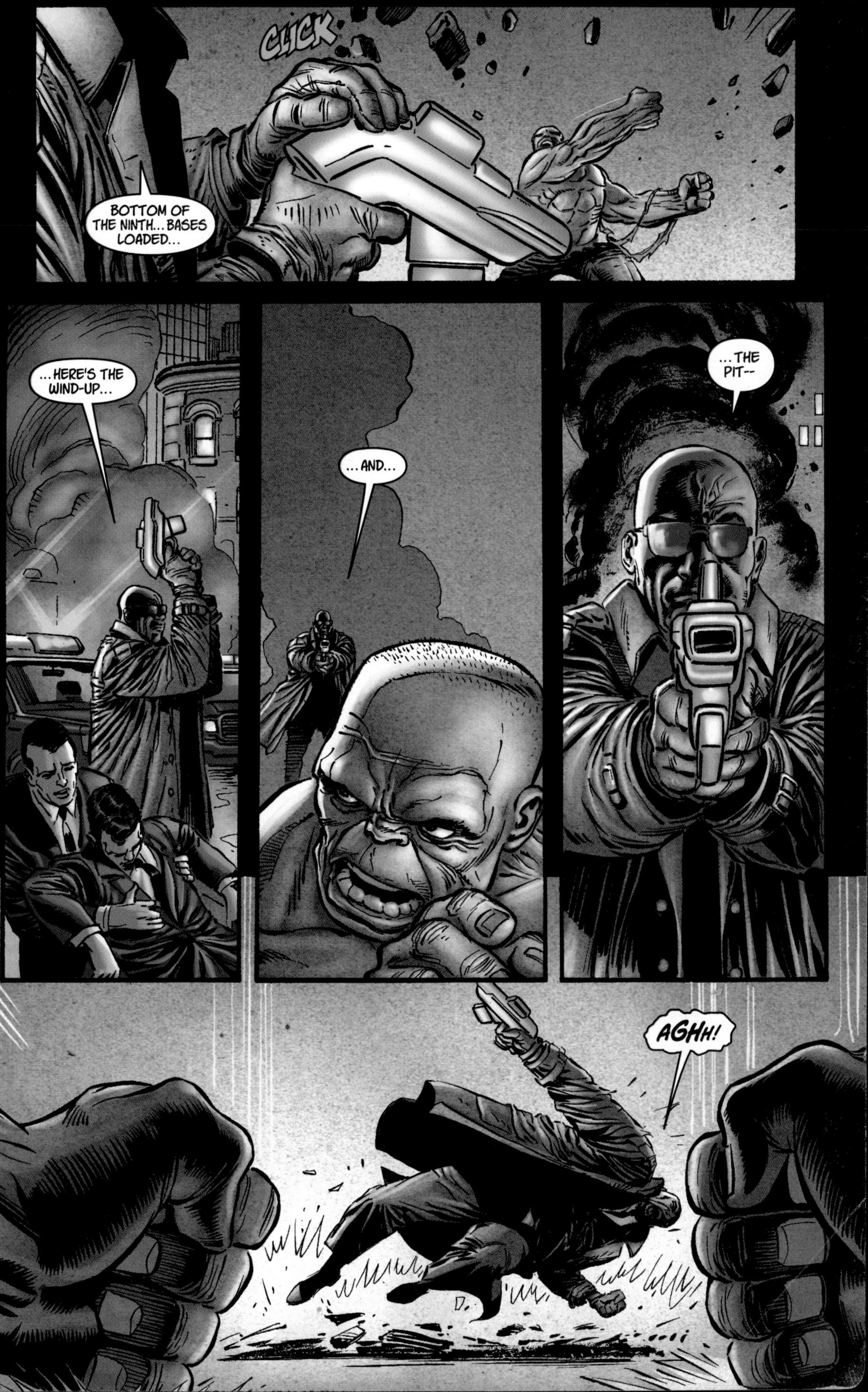
CLICK
BOTTOM OF THE NINTH... BASES LOADED...
...HERE'S THE WIND-UP...
...AND...
...THE PIT--
AGHH!

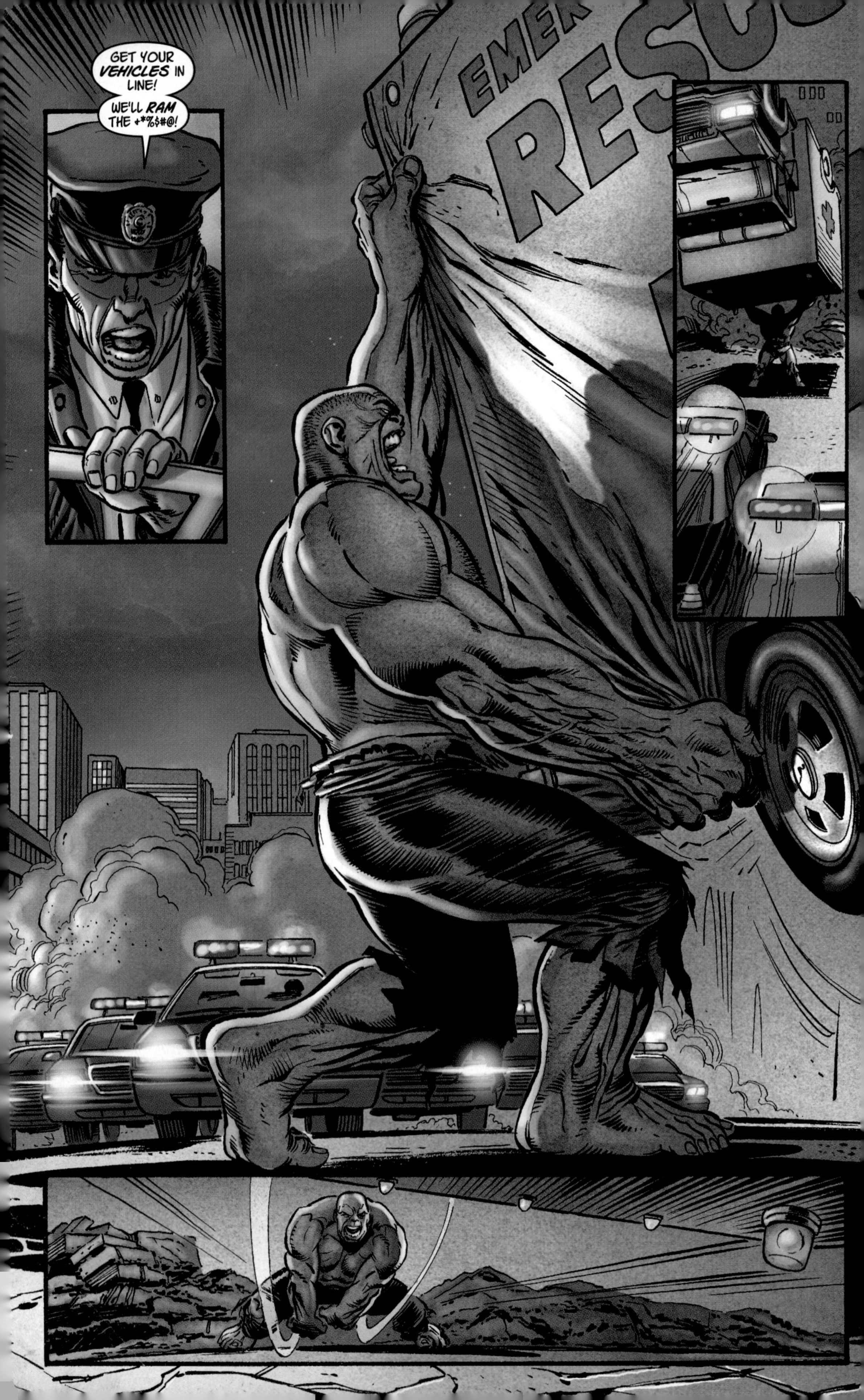
GET YOUR VEHICLES IN LINE!
WE'LL RAM THE +*%$#@!
EMER
RESC

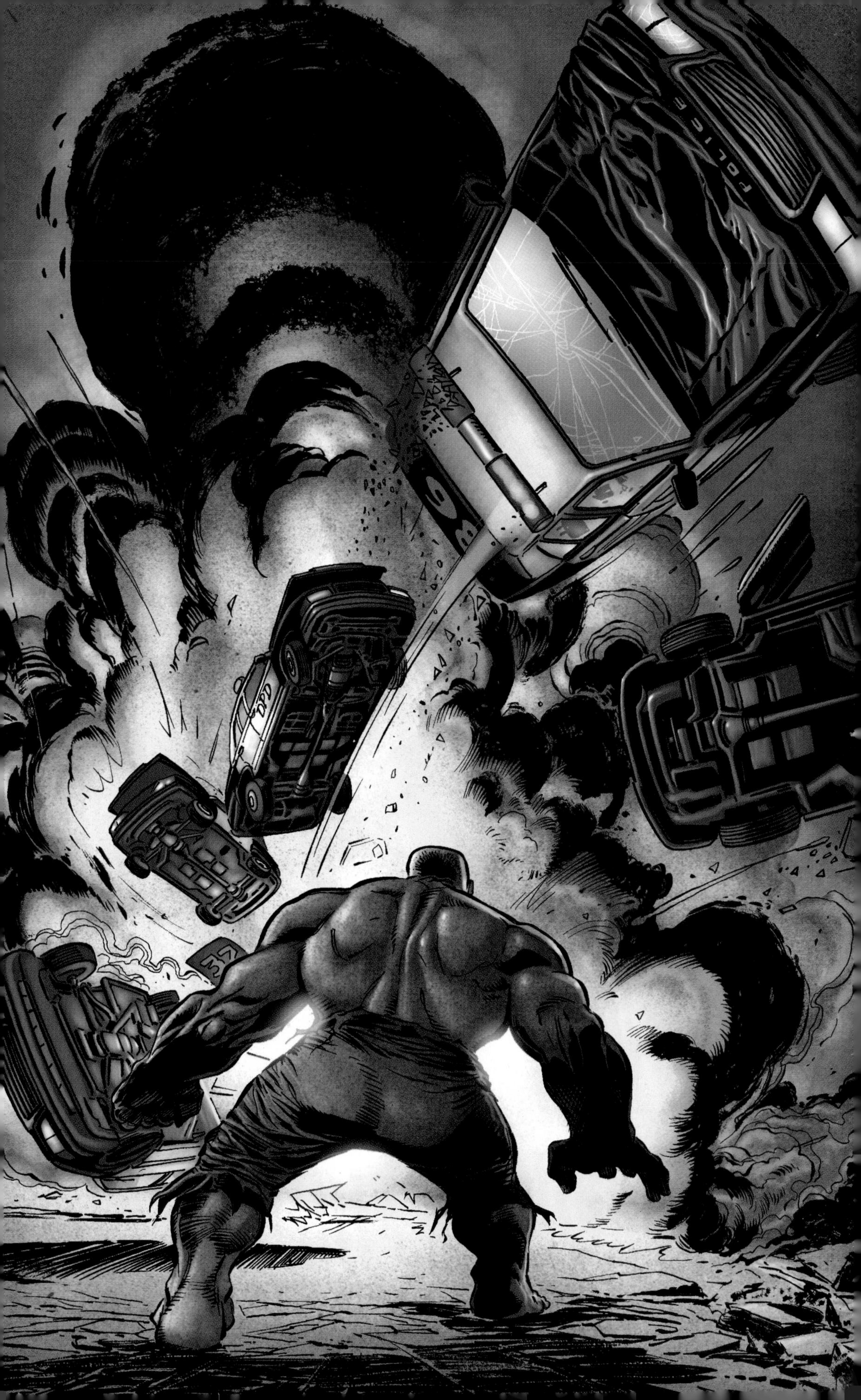
POLICE
DPD

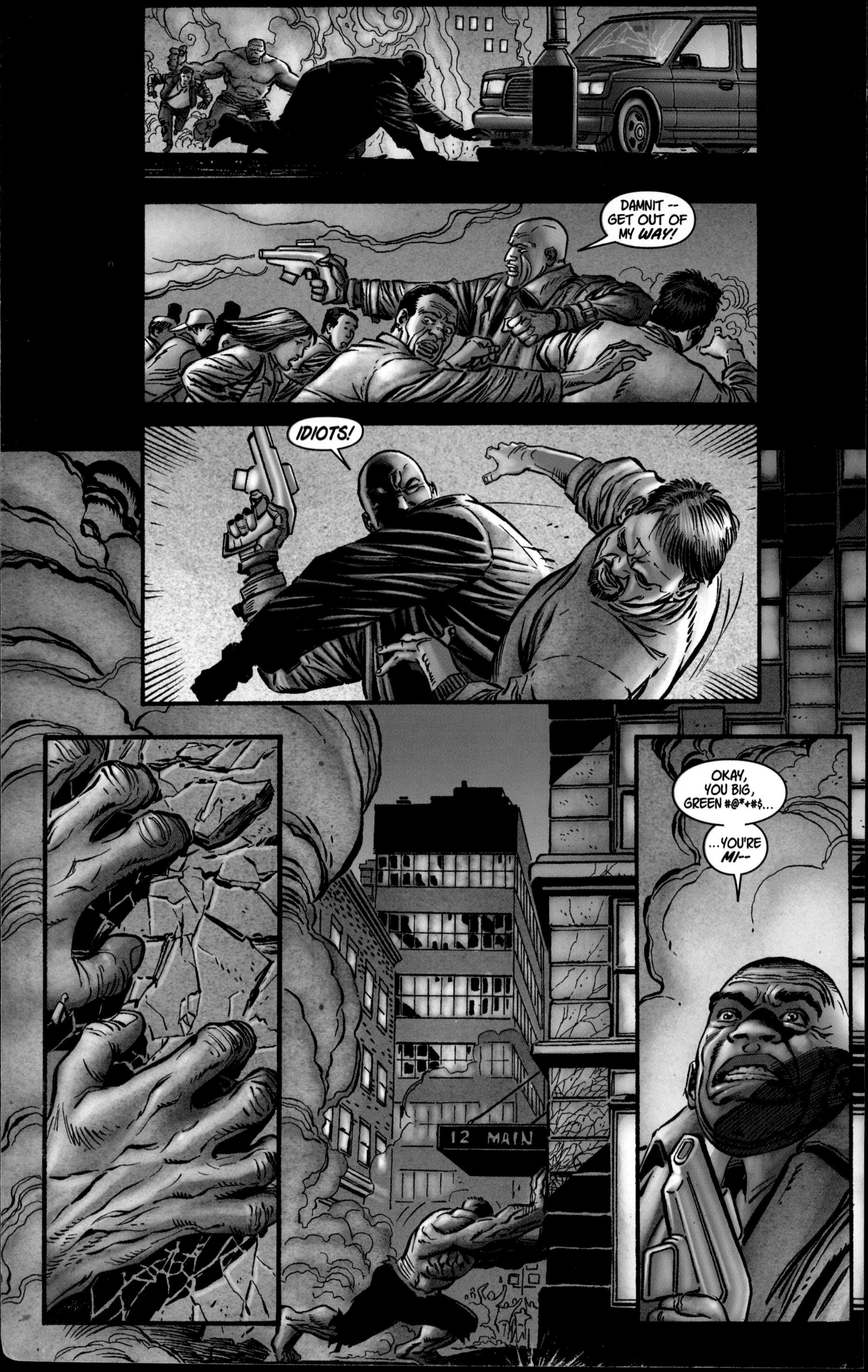
DAMNIT -- GET OUT OF MY WAY!
IDIOTS!
12 MAIN
OKAY, YOU BIG, GREEN #@*+#$...
...YOU'RE MI--

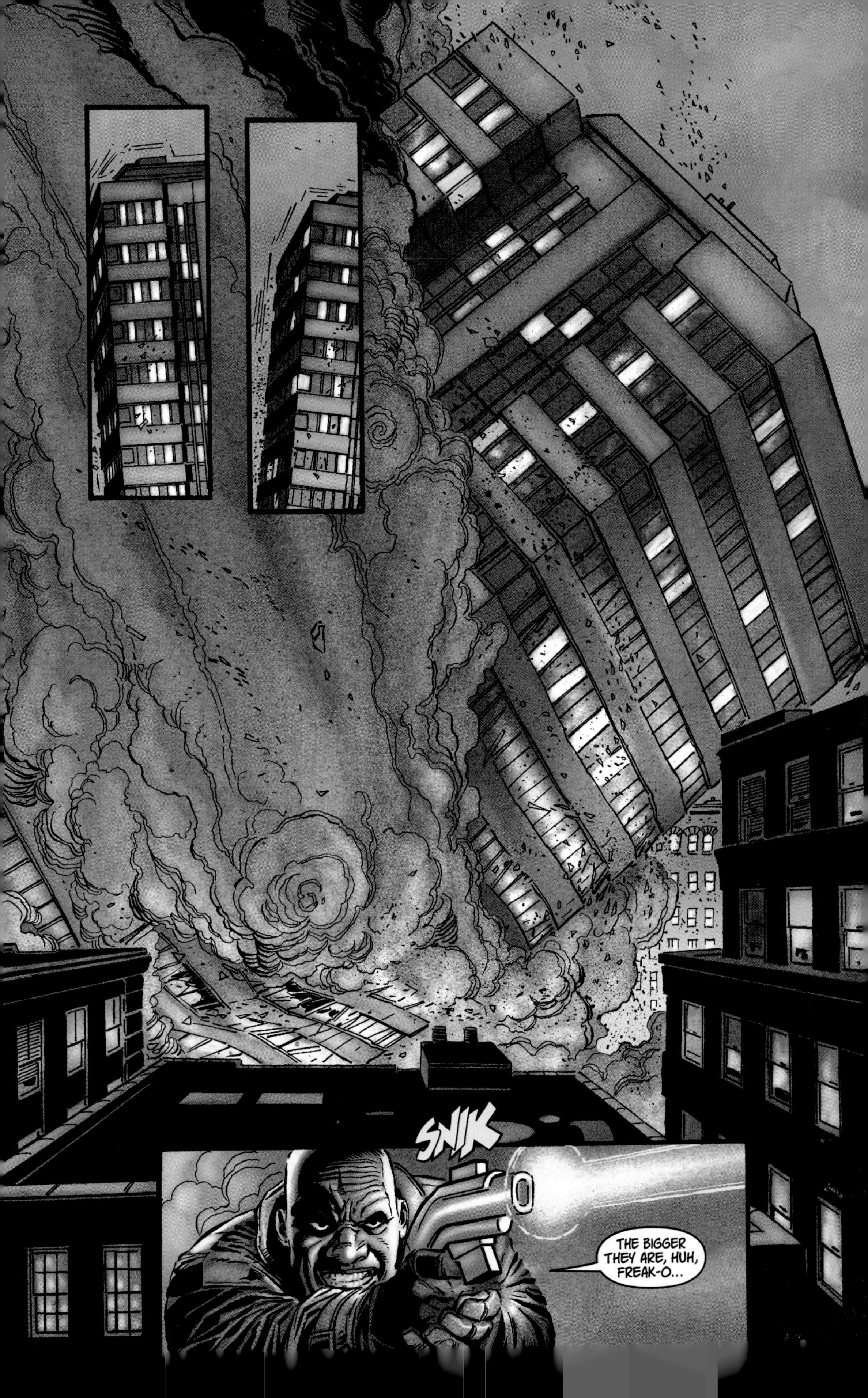
SNIK
THE BIGGER THEY ARE, HUH, FREAK-O...

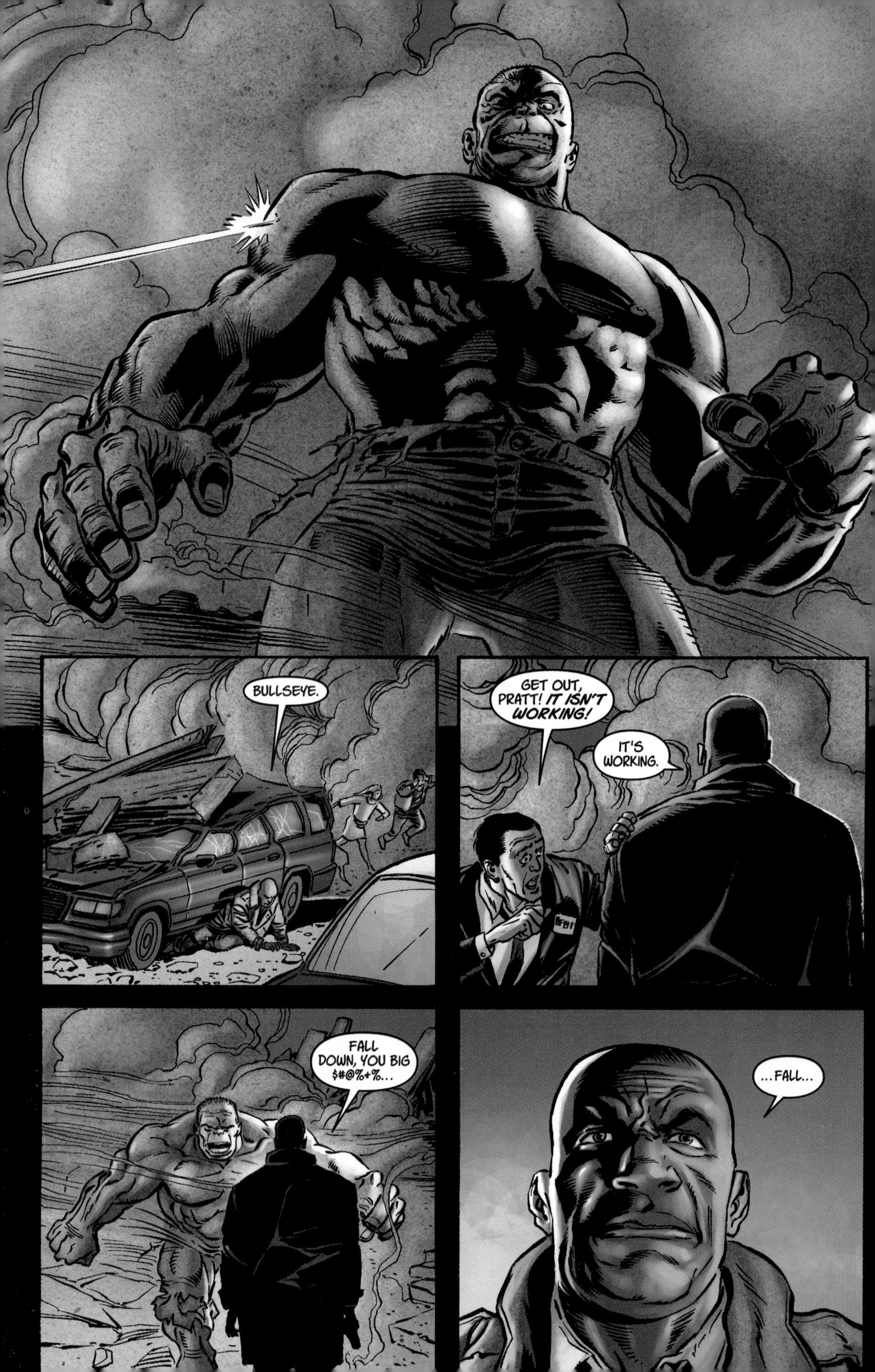
BULLSEYE.
GET OUT, PRATT! *IT ISN'T WORKING!*
IT'S WORKING.
FBI
FALL DOWN, YOU BIG $#@%+%...
...FALL...

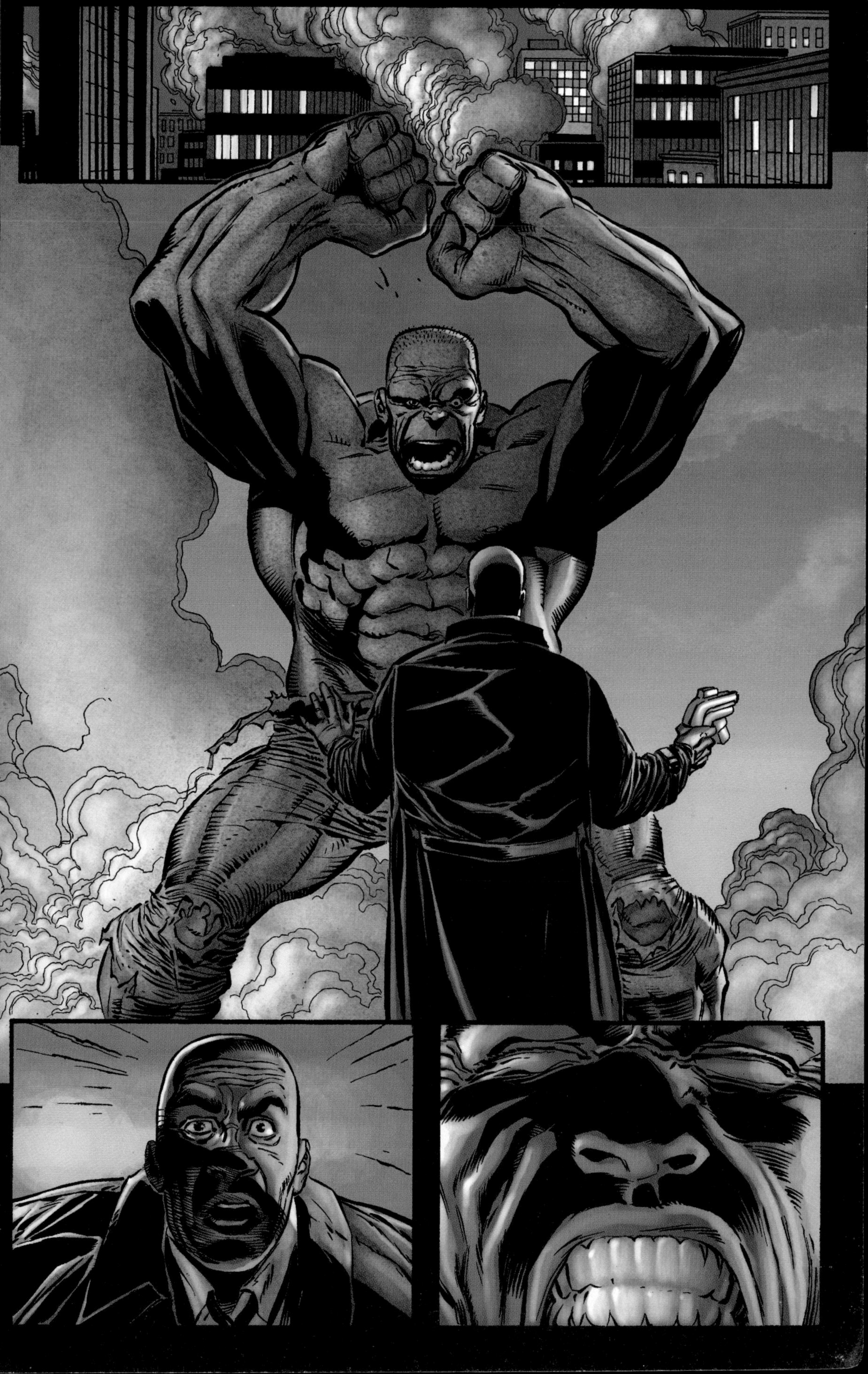

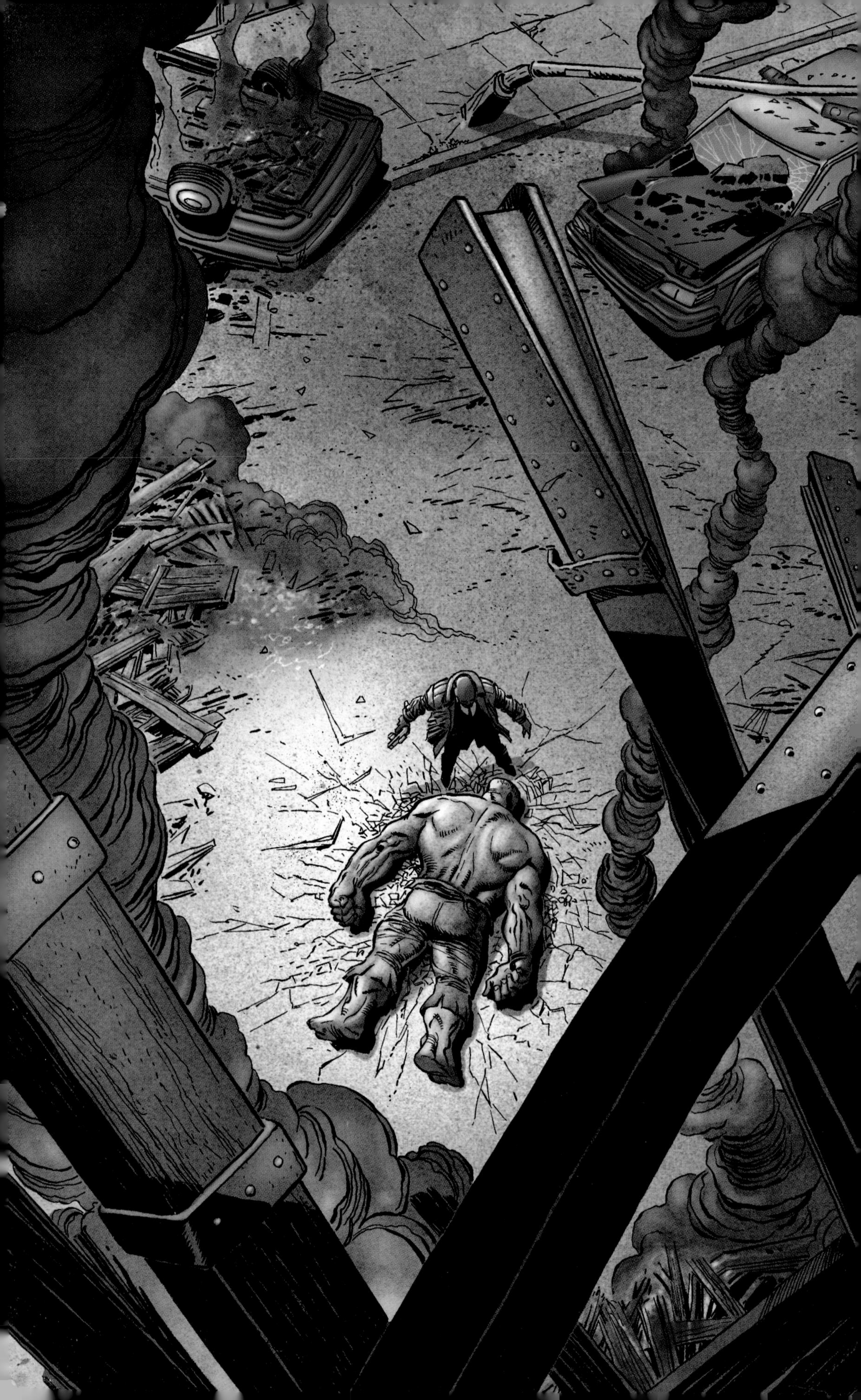

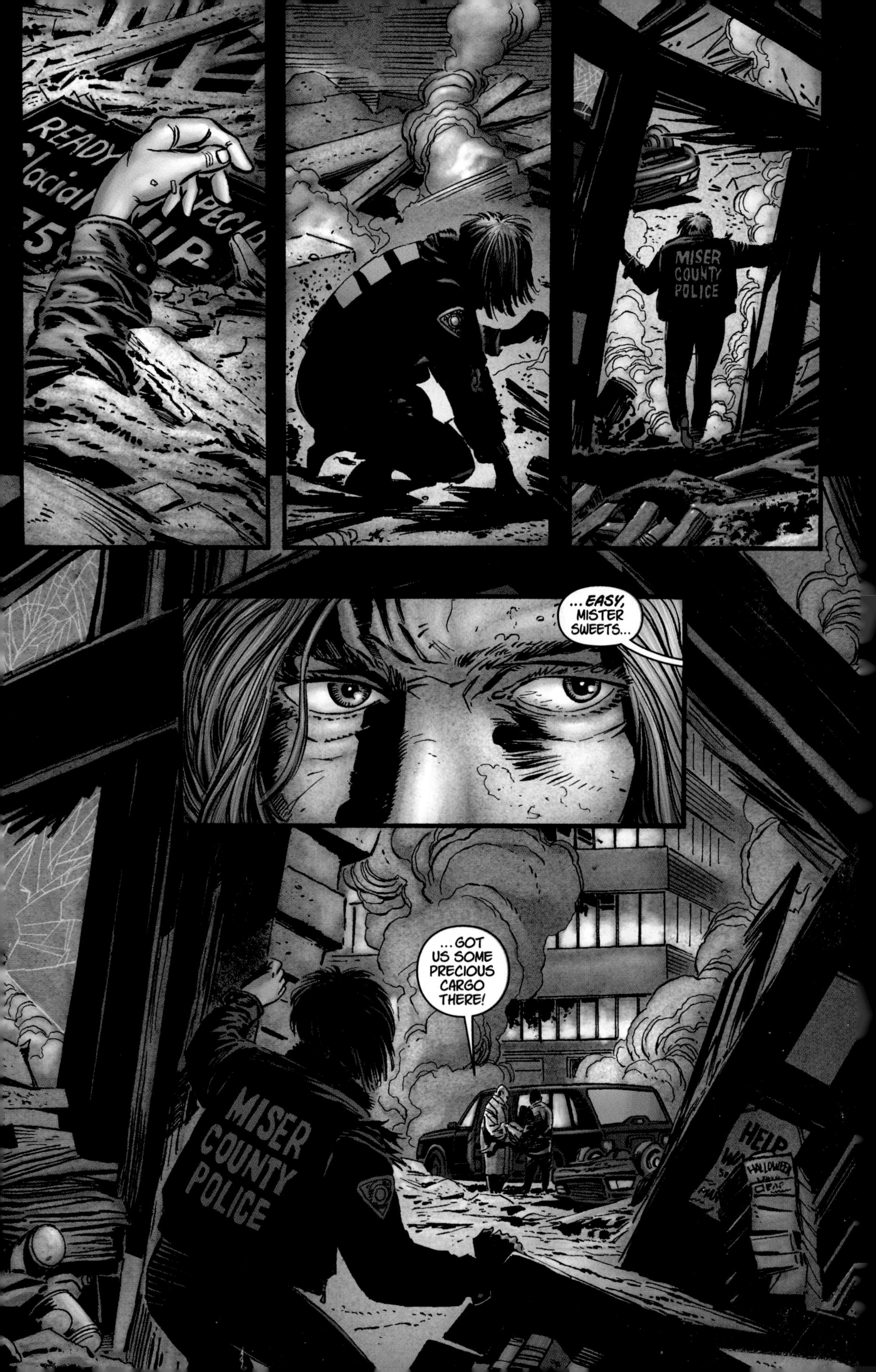
READY
Glacial
SPECI
75
MISER
COUNTY
POLICE
...EASY, MISTER SWEETS...
...GOT US SOME PRECIOUS CARGO THERE!
MISER
COUNTY
POLICE
HELP
HALLOWEEN

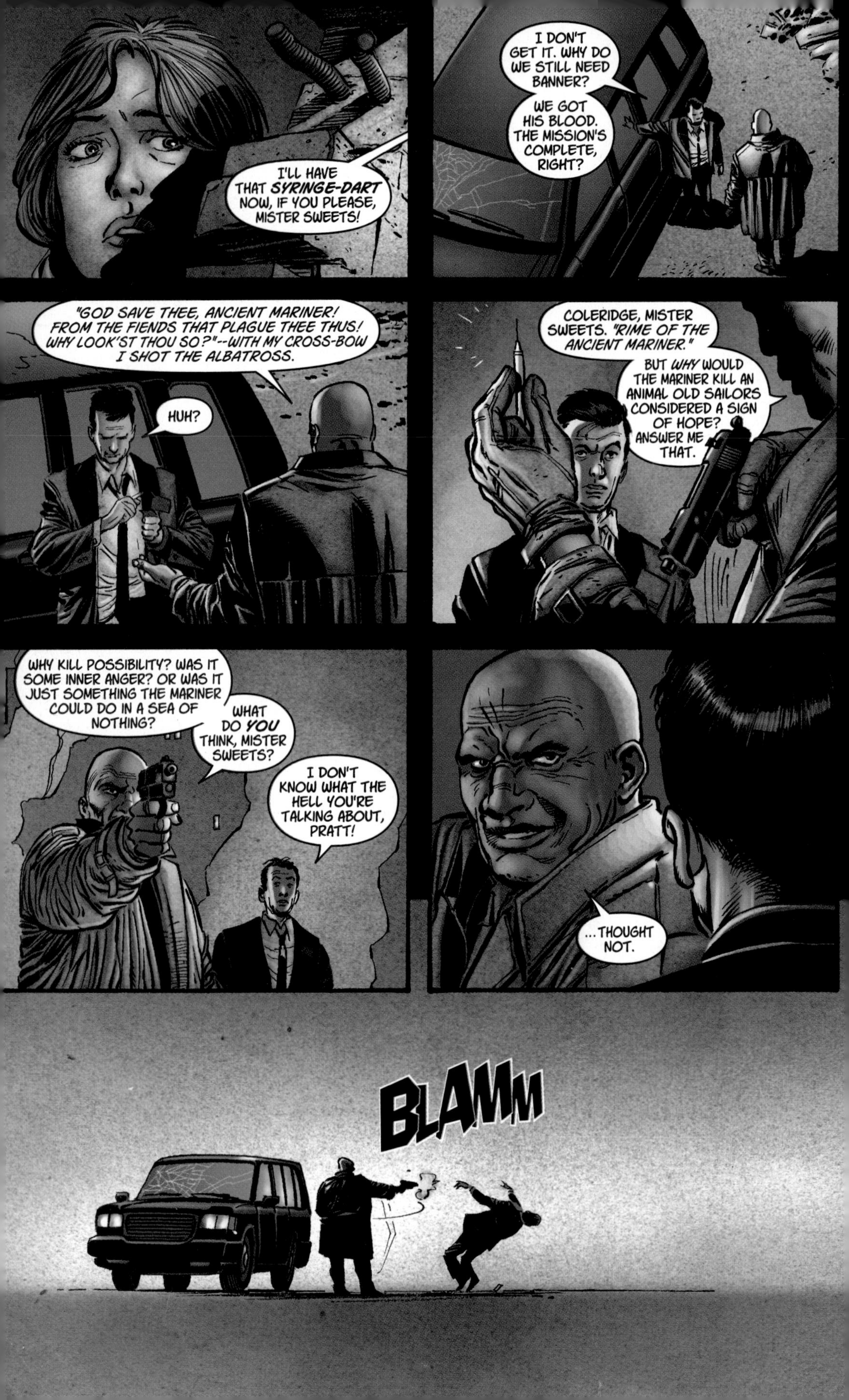
I'LL HAVE THAT SYRINGE-DART NOW, IF YOU PLEASE, MISTER SWEETS!
I DON'T GET IT. WHY DO WE STILL NEED BANNER?
WE GOT HIS BLOOD. THE MISSION'S COMPLETE, RIGHT?
"GOD SAVE THEE, ANCIENT MARINER! FROM THE FIENDS THAT PLAGUE THEE THUS! WHY LOOK'ST THOU SO?"--WITH MY CROSS-BOW I SHOT THE ALBATROSS.
HUH?
COLERIDGE, MISTER SWEETS. "RIME OF THE ANCIENT MARINER."
BUT WHY WOULD THE MARINER KILL AN ANIMAL OLD SAILORS CONSIDERED A SIGN OF HOPE? ANSWER ME THAT.
WHY KILL POSSIBILITY? WAS IT SOME INNER ANGER? OR WAS IT JUST SOMETHING THE MARINER COULD DO IN A SEA OF NOTHING?
WHAT DO YOU THINK, MISTER SWEETS?
I DON'T KNOW WHAT THE HELL YOU'RE TALKING ABOUT, PRATT!
...THOUGHT NOT.
BLAMM

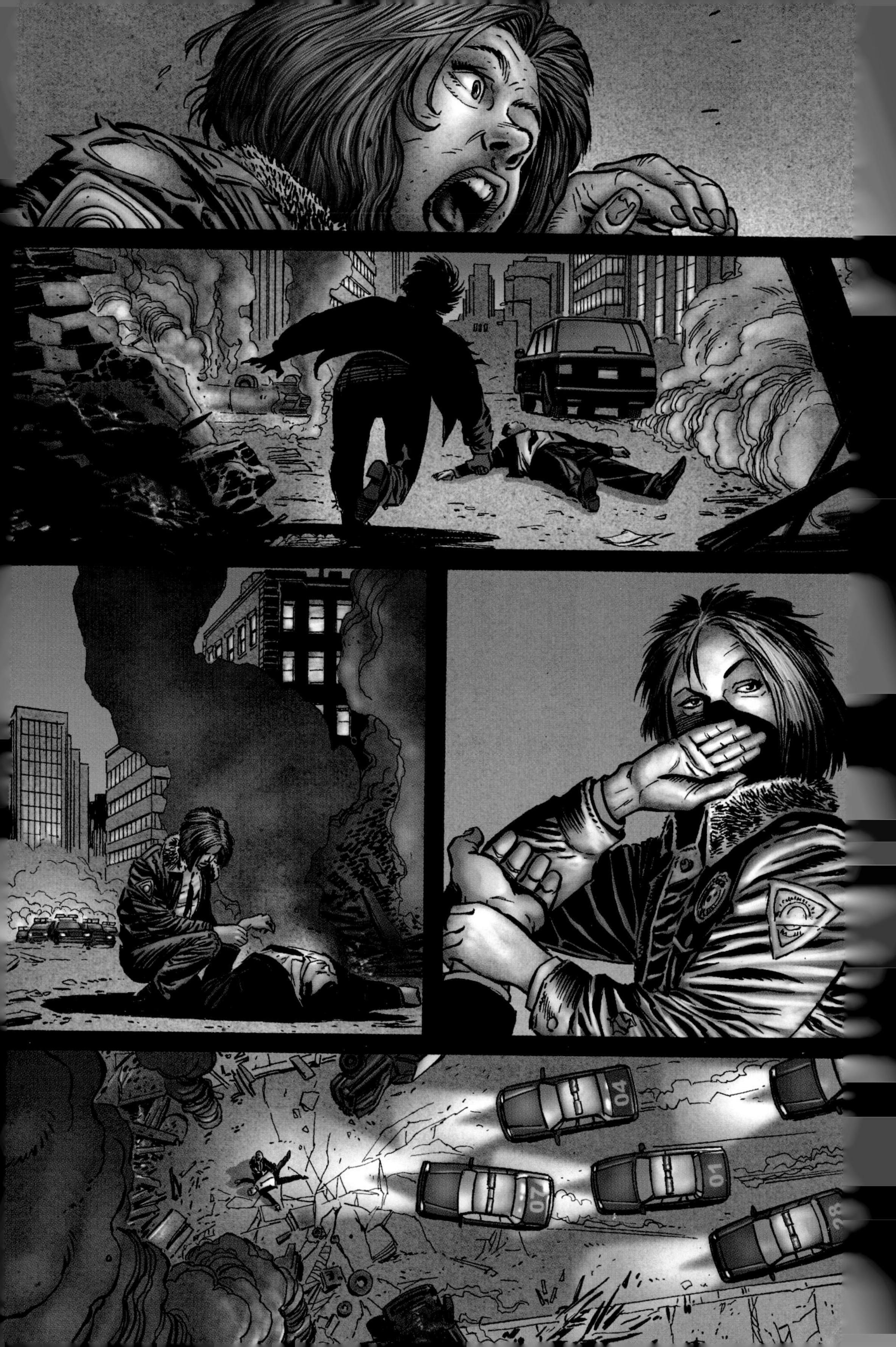
04
07
01

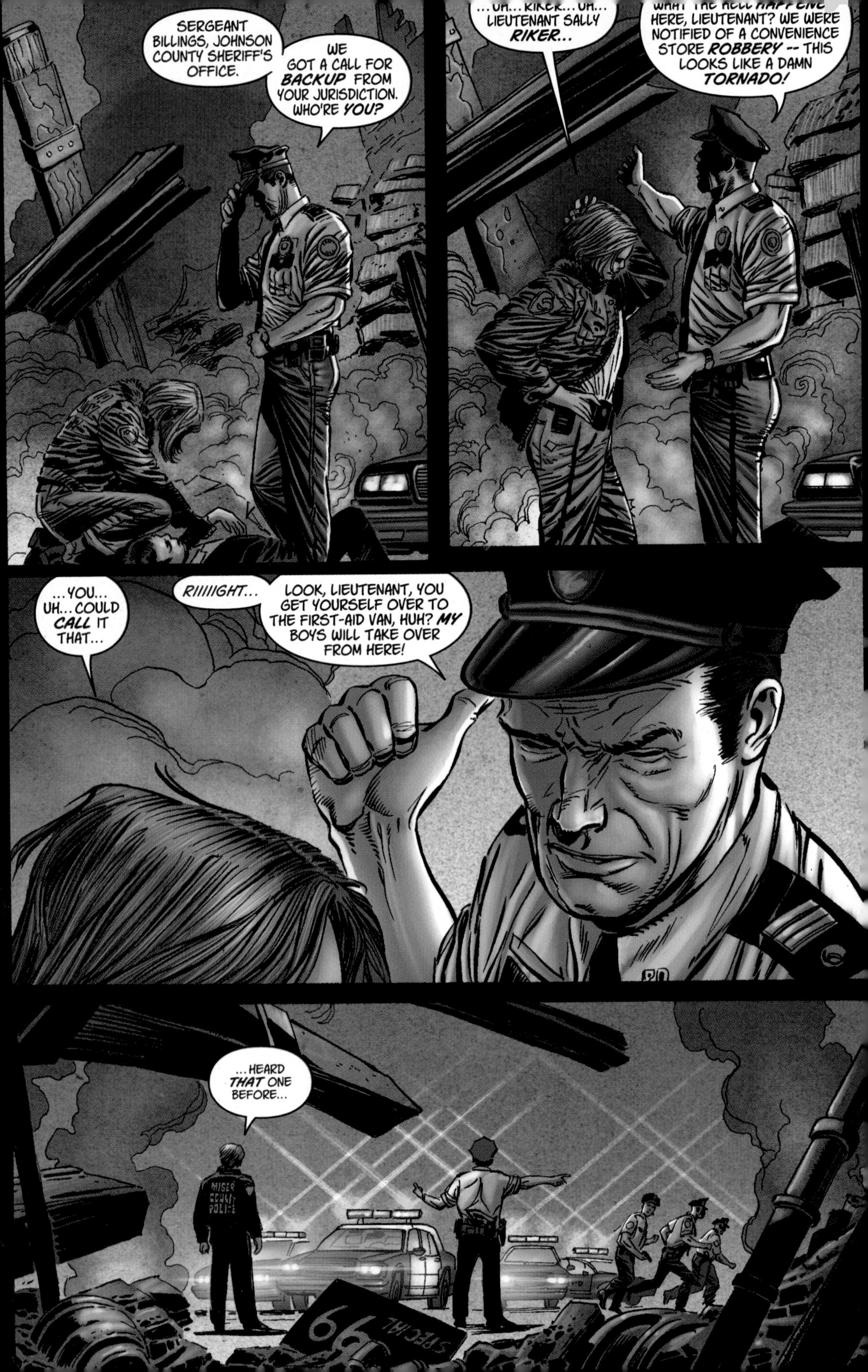

SERGEANT BILLINGS, JOHNSON COUNTY SHERIFF'S OFFICE.
WE GOT A CALL FOR BACKUP FROM YOUR JURISDICTION. WHO'RE YOU?
...UH...RIKER...UH... LIEUTENANT SALLY RIKER...
HERE, LIEUTENANT? WE WERE NOTIFIED OF A CONVENIENCE STORE ROBBERY -- THIS LOOKS LIKE A DAMN TORNADO!
...YOU... UH...COULD CALL IT THAT...
RIIIIIGHT...
LOOK, LIEUTENANT, YOU GET YOURSELF OVER TO THE FIRST-AID VAN, HUH? MY BOYS WILL TAKE OVER FROM HERE!
...HEARD THAT ONE BEFORE...

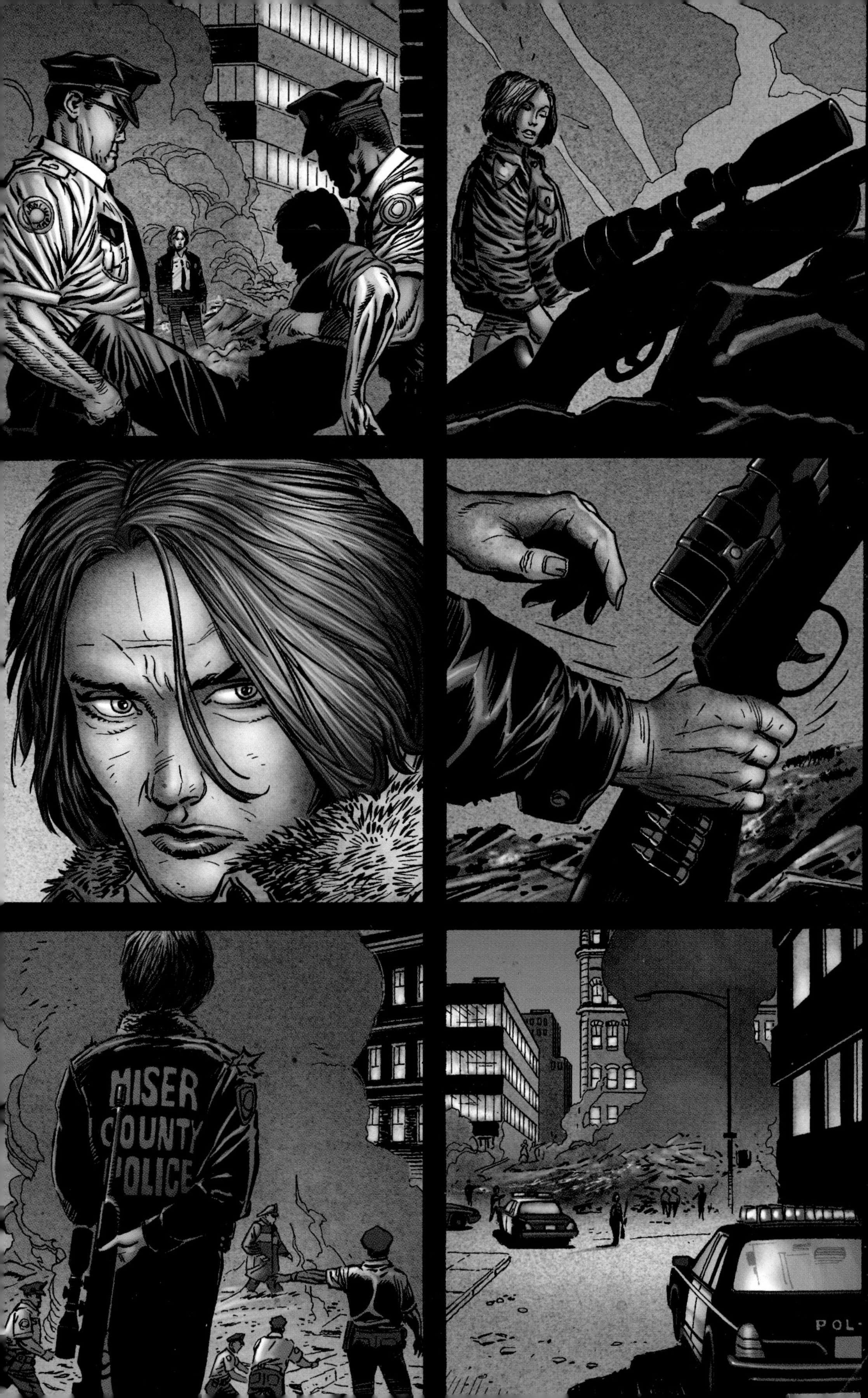
MISER COUNTY POLICE
POL-

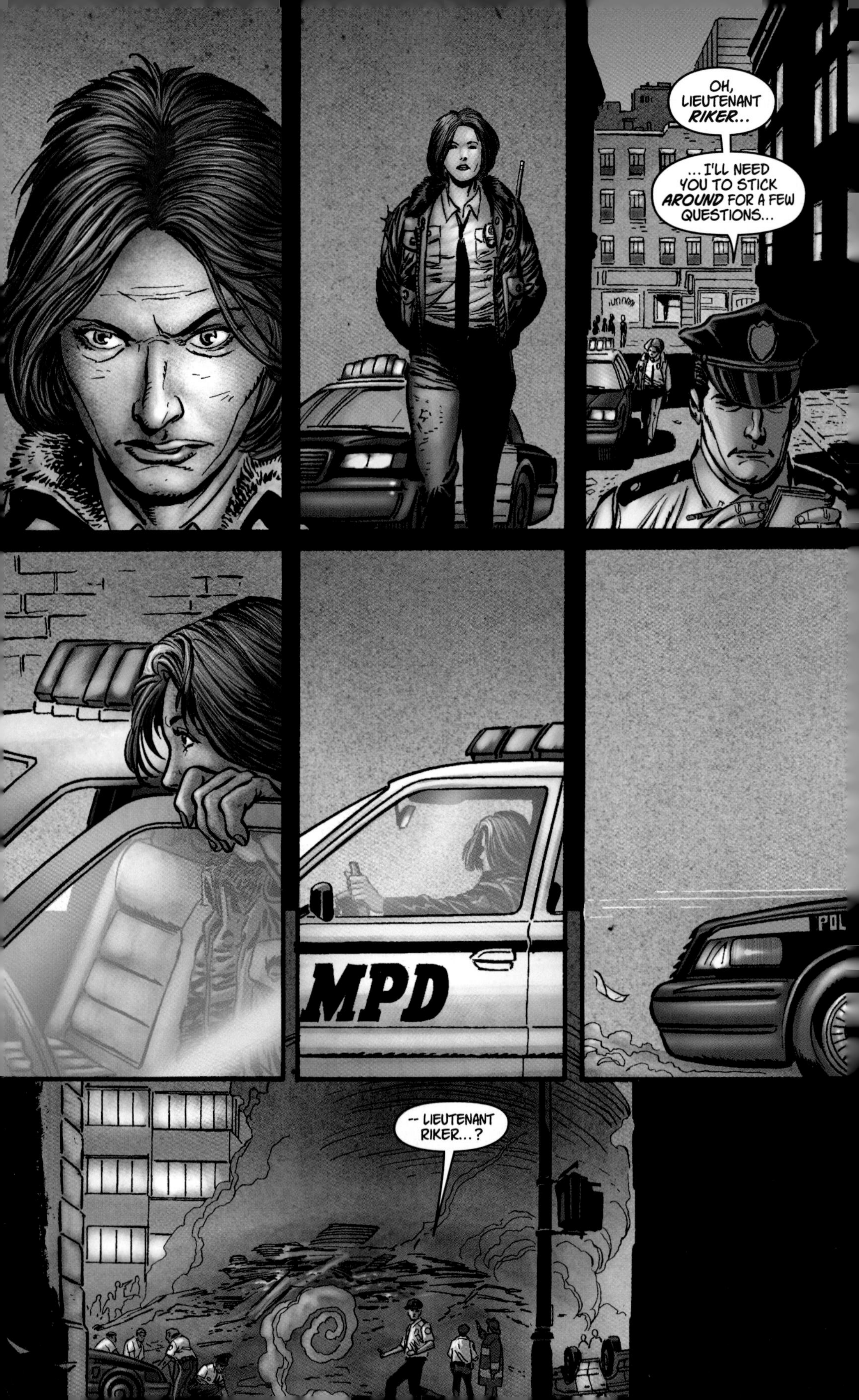
OH, LIEUTENANT RIKER...
...I'LL NEED YOU TO STICK AROUND FOR A FEW QUESTIONS...
MPD
POL
-- LIEUTENANT RIKER...?

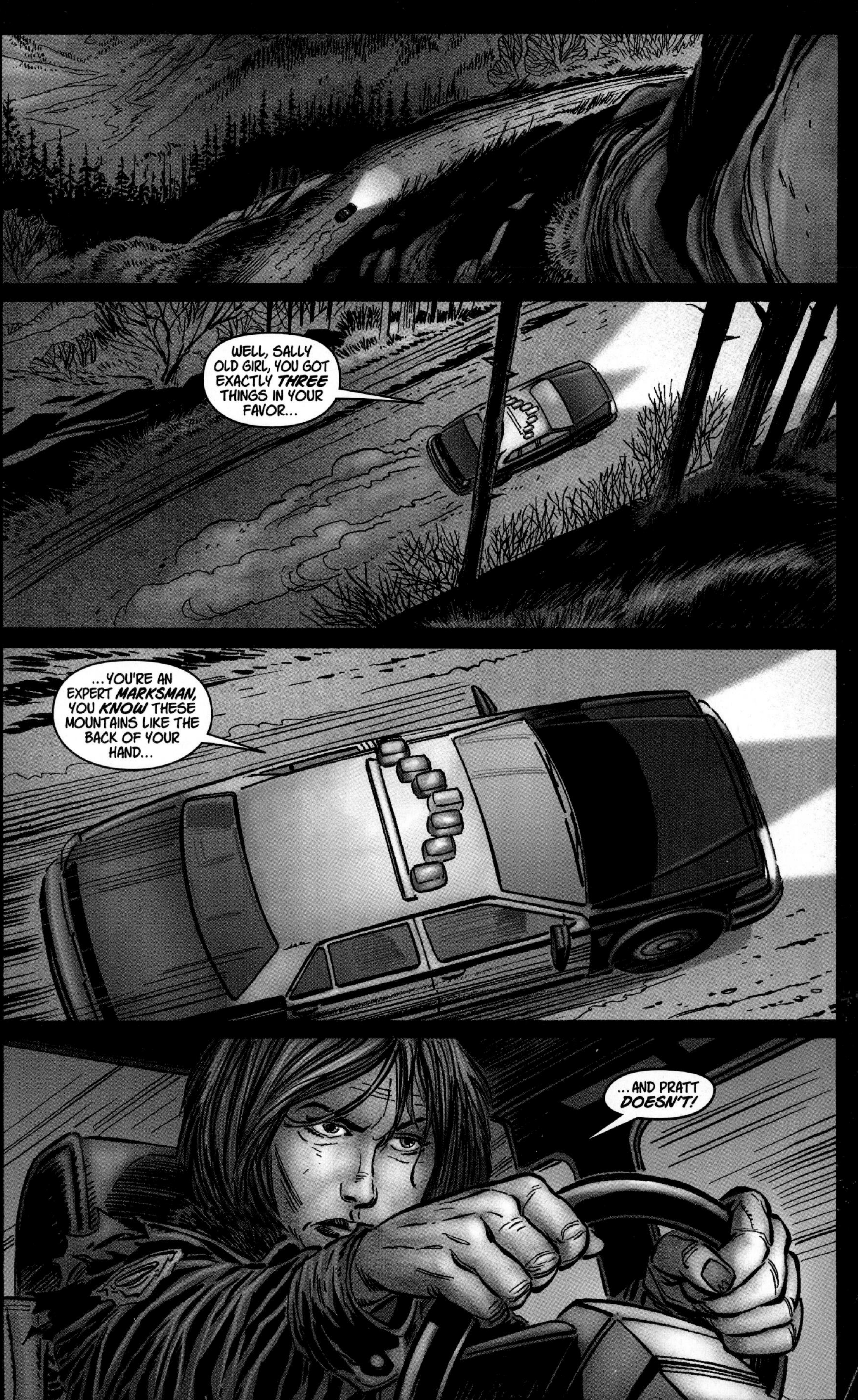
WELL, SALLY OLD GIRL, YOU GOT EXACTLY THREE THINGS IN YOUR FAVOR...
...YOU'RE AN EXPERT MARKSMAN, YOU KNOW THESE MOUNTAINS LIKE THE BACK OF YOUR HAND...
...AND PRATT DOESN'T!

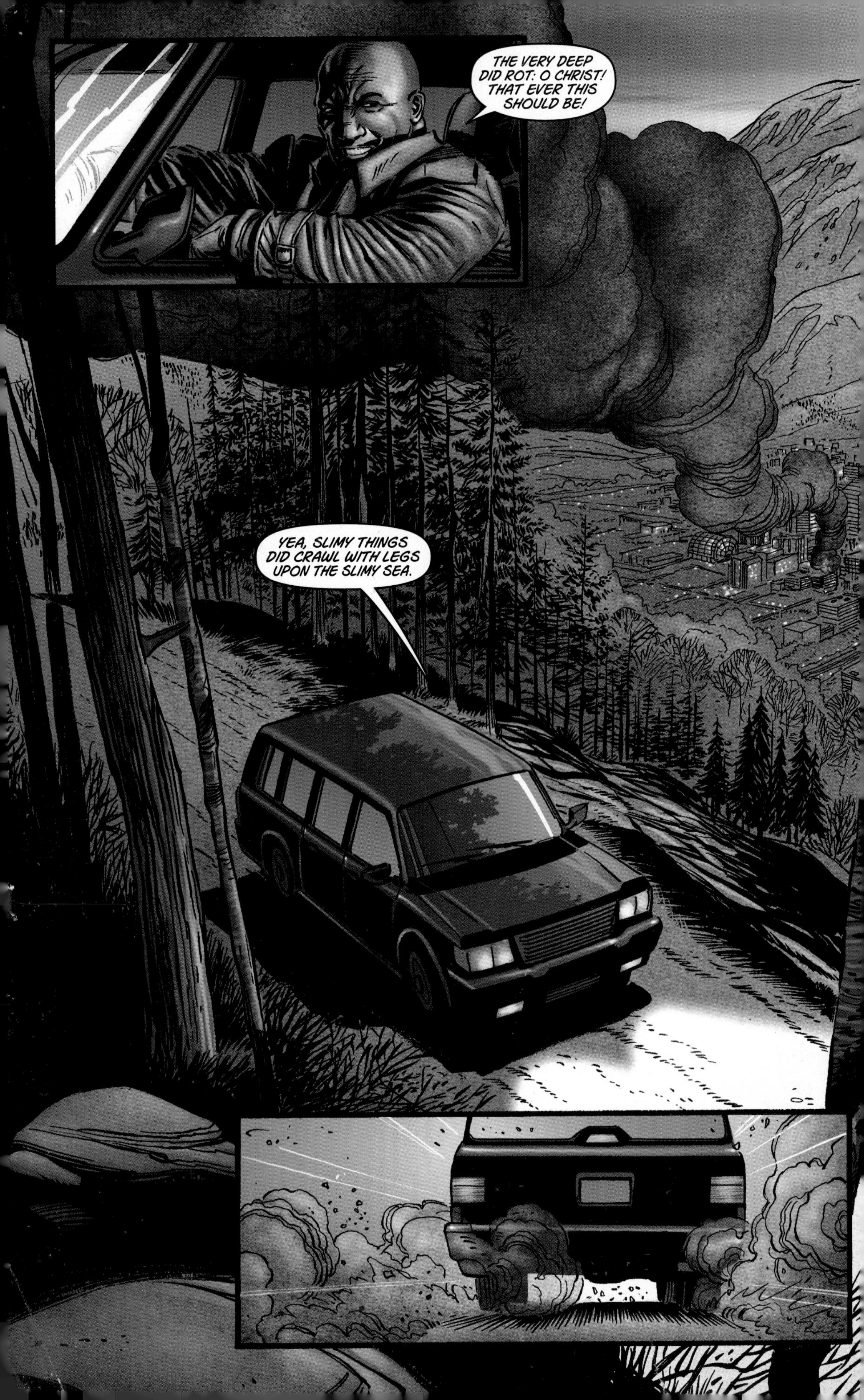
THE VERY DEEP DID ROT: O CHRIST! THAT EVER THIS SHOULD BE!
YEA, SLIMY THINGS DID CRAWL WITH LEGS UPON THE SLIMY SEA.

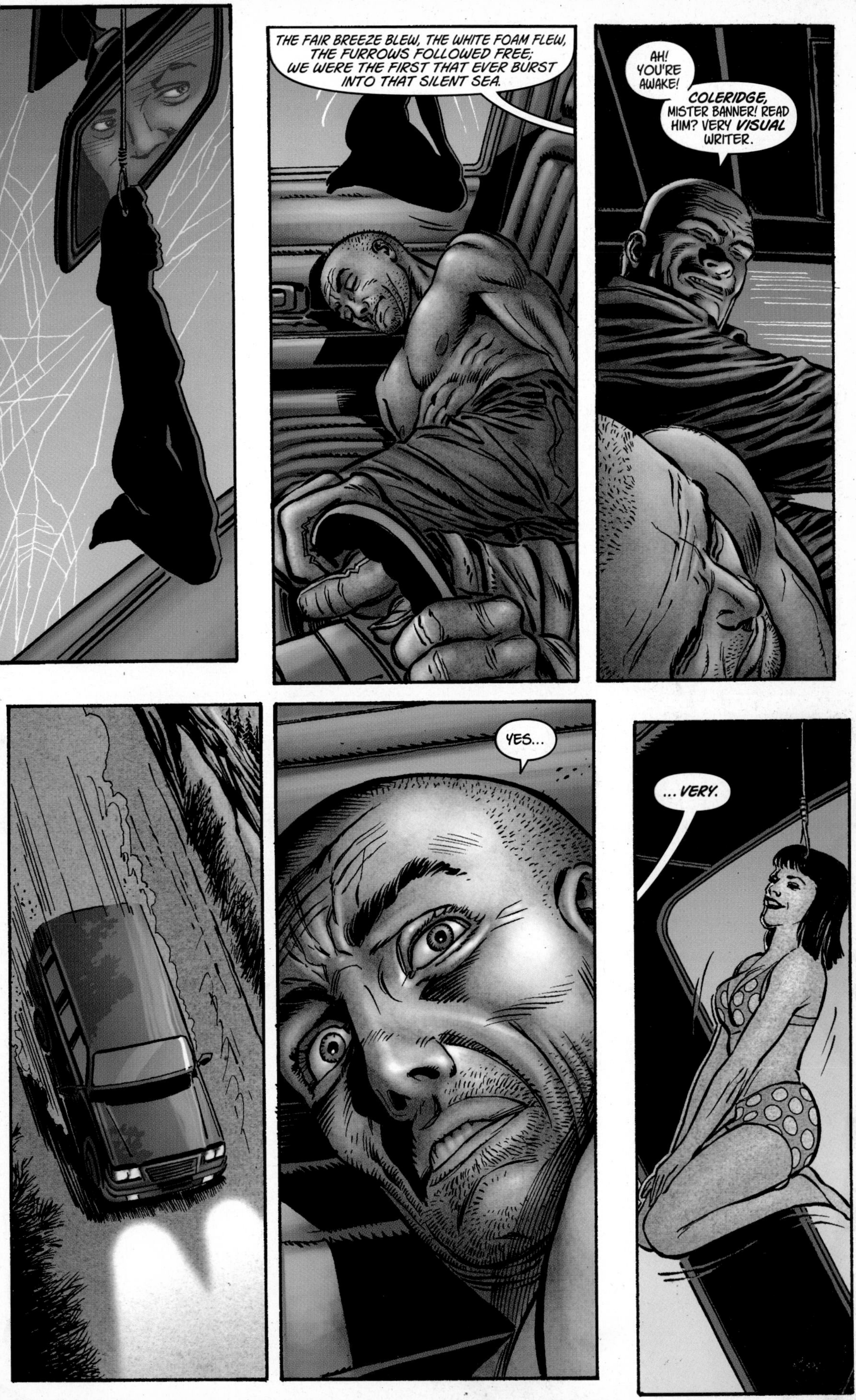
THE FAIR BREEZE BLEW, THE WHITE FOAM FLEW, THE FURROWS FOLLOWED FREE; WE WERE THE FIRST THAT EVER BURST INTO THAT SILENT SEA.
AH! YOU'RE AWAKE!
COLERIDGE, MISTER BANNER! READ HIM? VERY VISUAL WRITER.
YES...
...VERY.

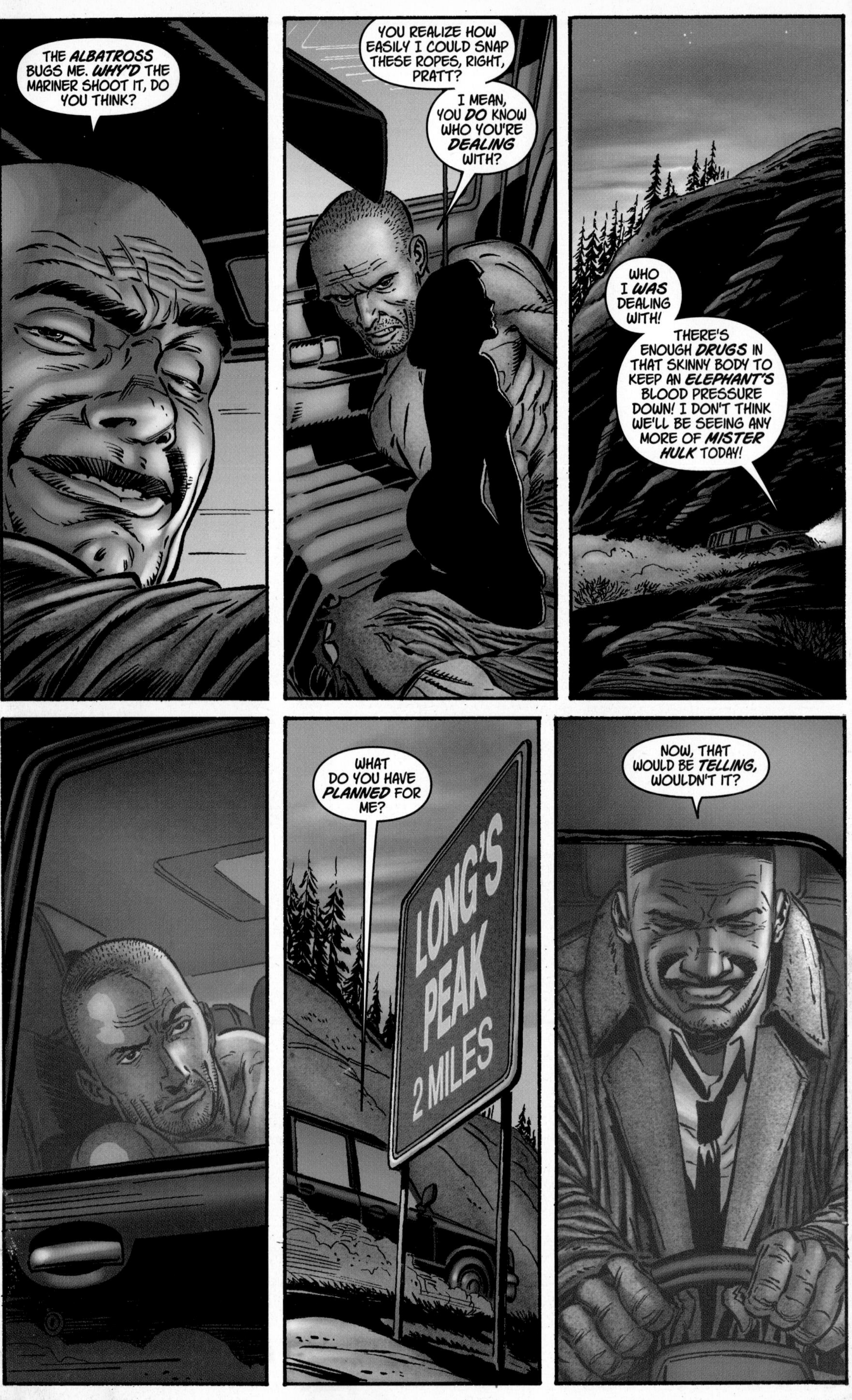

THE ALBATROSS BUGS ME. WHY'D THE MARINER SHOOT IT, DO YOU THINK?
YOU REALIZE HOW EASILY I COULD SNAP THESE ROPES, RIGHT, PRATT?
I MEAN, YOU DO KNOW WHO YOU'RE DEALING WITH?
WHO I WAS DEALING WITH!
THERE'S ENOUGH DRUGS IN THAT SKINNY BODY TO KEEP AN ELEPHANT'S BLOOD PRESSURE DOWN! I DON'T THINK WE'LL BE SEEING ANY MORE OF MISTER HULK TODAY!
WHAT DO YOU HAVE PLANNED FOR ME?
LONG'S PEAK 2 MILES
NOW, THAT WOULD BE TELLING, WOULDN'T IT?

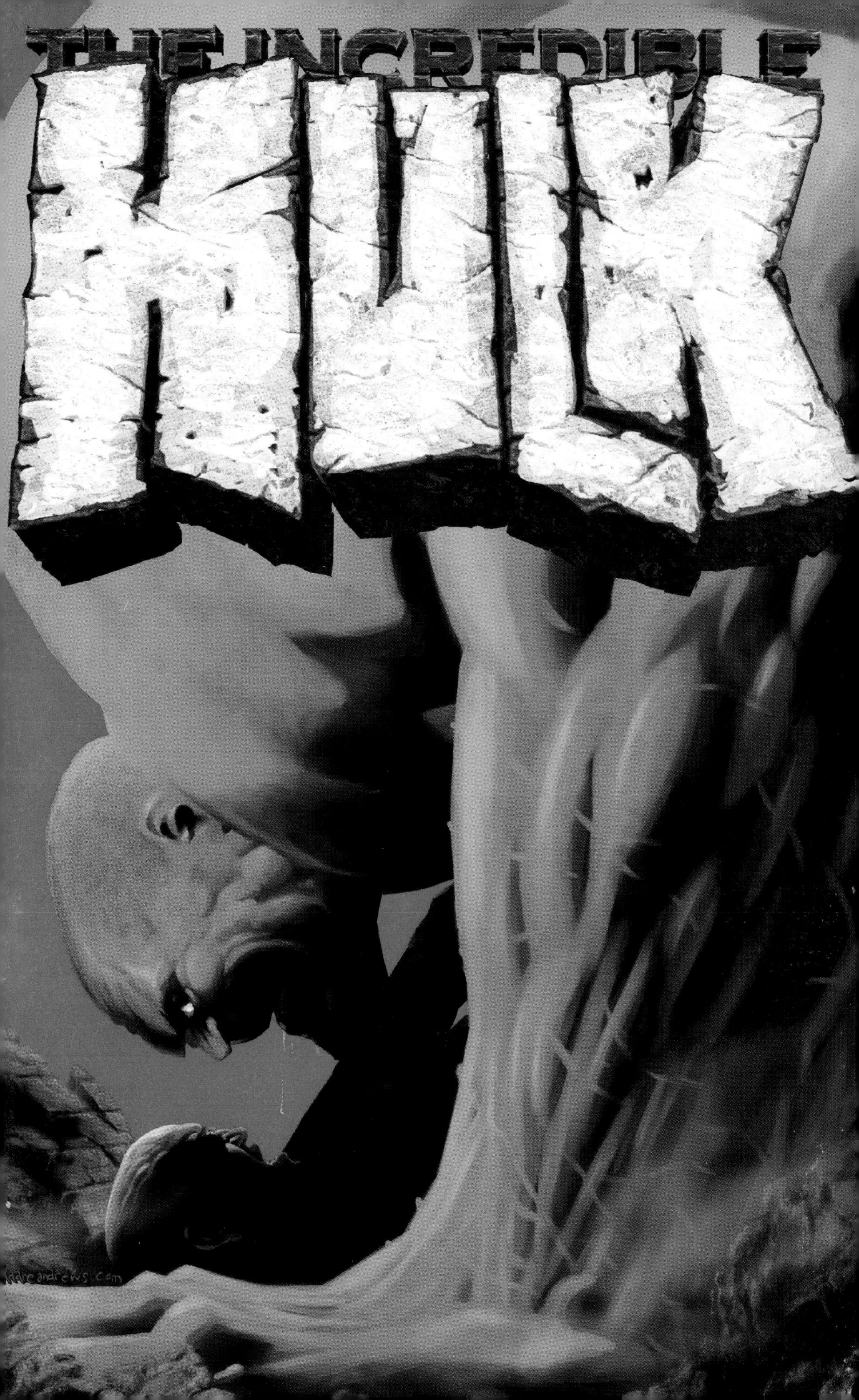
THE INCREDIBLE
HULK

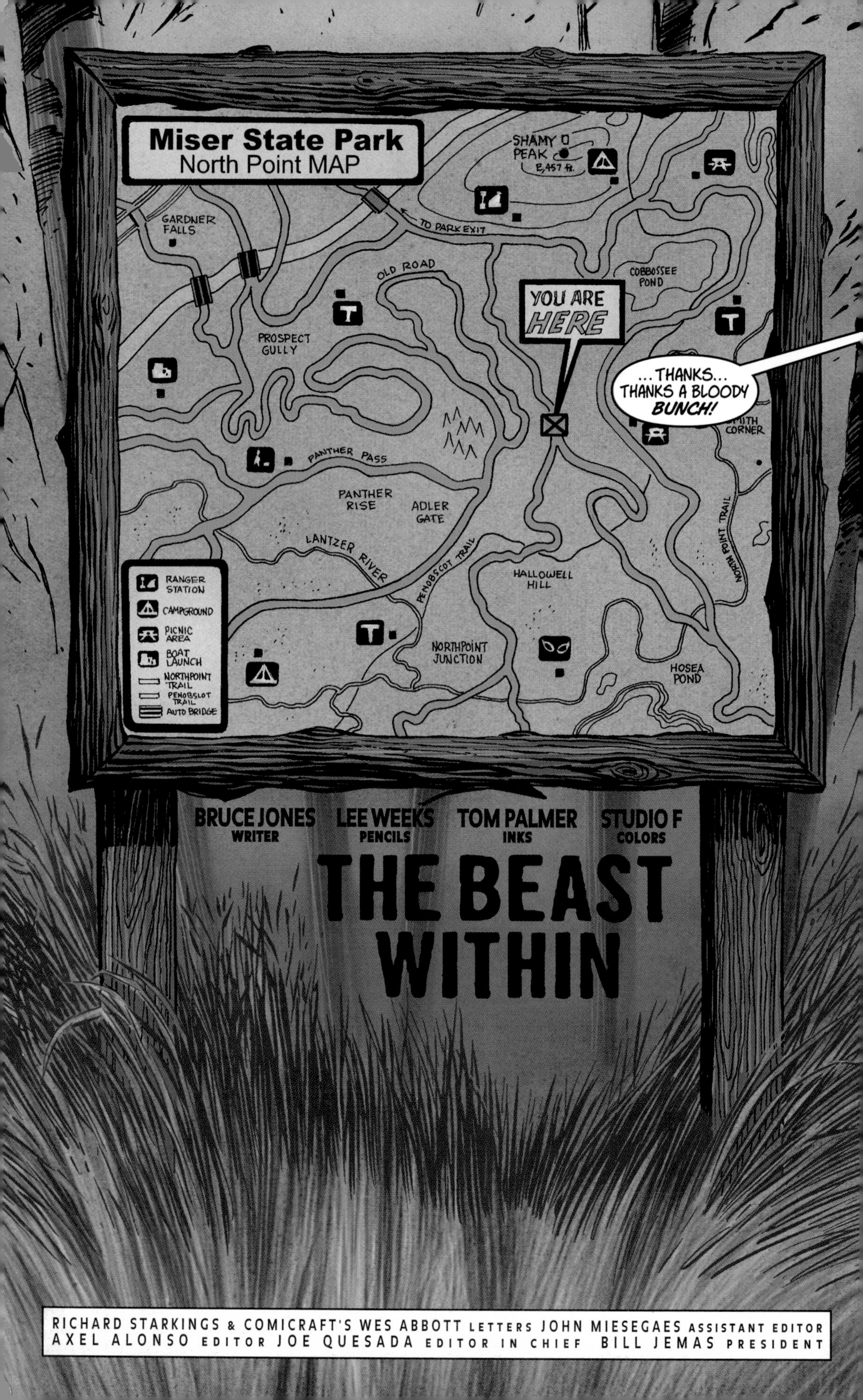
Miser State Park
North Point MAP
SHAMY PEAK
8,457 ft.
GARDNER FALLS
TO PARK EXIT
OLD ROAD
COBBOSSEE POND
YOU ARE HERE
PROSPECT GULLY
...THANKS... THANKS A BLOODY BUNCH!
SMITH CORNER
PANTHER PASS
PANTHER RISE
ADLER GATE
LANTZER RIVER
PENOBSCOT TRAIL
HALLOWELL HILL
NORTH POINT TRAIL
NORTHPOINT JUNCTION
HOSEA POND
RANGER STATION
CAMPGROUND
PICNIC AREA
BOAT LAUNCH
NORTHPOINT TRAIL
PENOBSLOT TRAIL
AUTO BRIDGE
BRUCE JONES WRITER
LEE WEEKS PENCILS
TOM PALMER INKS
STUDIO F COLORS
THE BEAST WITHIN
RICHARD STARKINGS & COMICRAFT'S WES ABBOTT LETTERS JOHN MIESEGAES ASSISTANT EDITOR
AXEL ALONSO EDITOR JOE QUESADA EDITOR IN CHIEF BILL JEMAS PRESIDENT

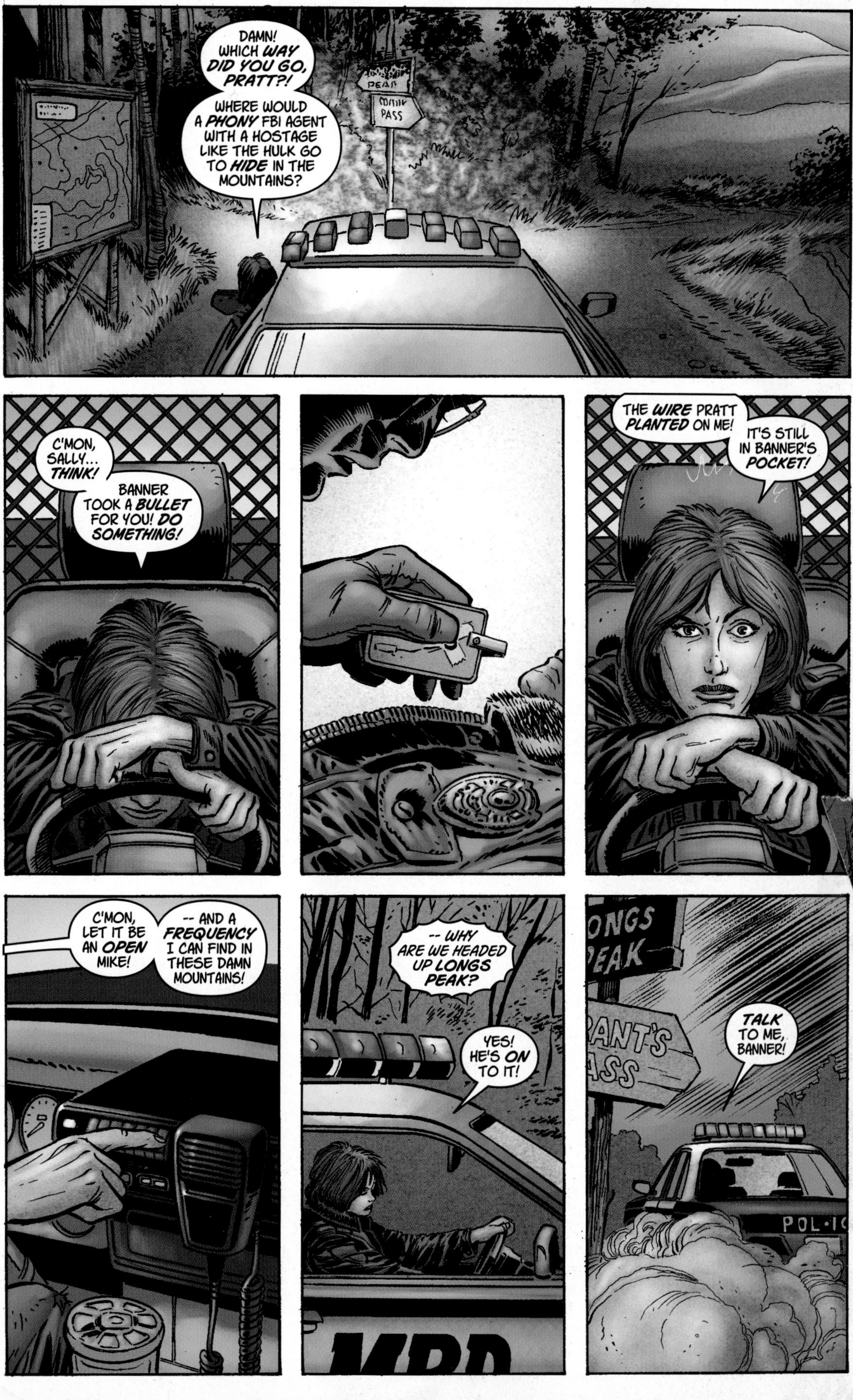
DAMN! WHICH WAY DID YOU GO, PRATT?!
WHERE WOULD A PHONY FBI AGENT WITH A HOSTAGE LIKE THE HULK GO TO HIDE IN THE MOUNTAINS?
C'MON, SALLY... THINK!
BANNER TOOK A BULLET FOR YOU! DO SOMETHING!
THE WIRE PRATT PLANTED ON ME!
IT'S STILL IN BANNER'S POCKET!
C'MON, LET IT BE AN OPEN MIKE!
-- AND A FREQUENCY I CAN FIND IN THESE DAMN MOUNTAINS!
-- WHY ARE WE HEADED UP LONGS PEAK?
YES! HE'S ON TO IT!
TALK TO ME, BANNER!

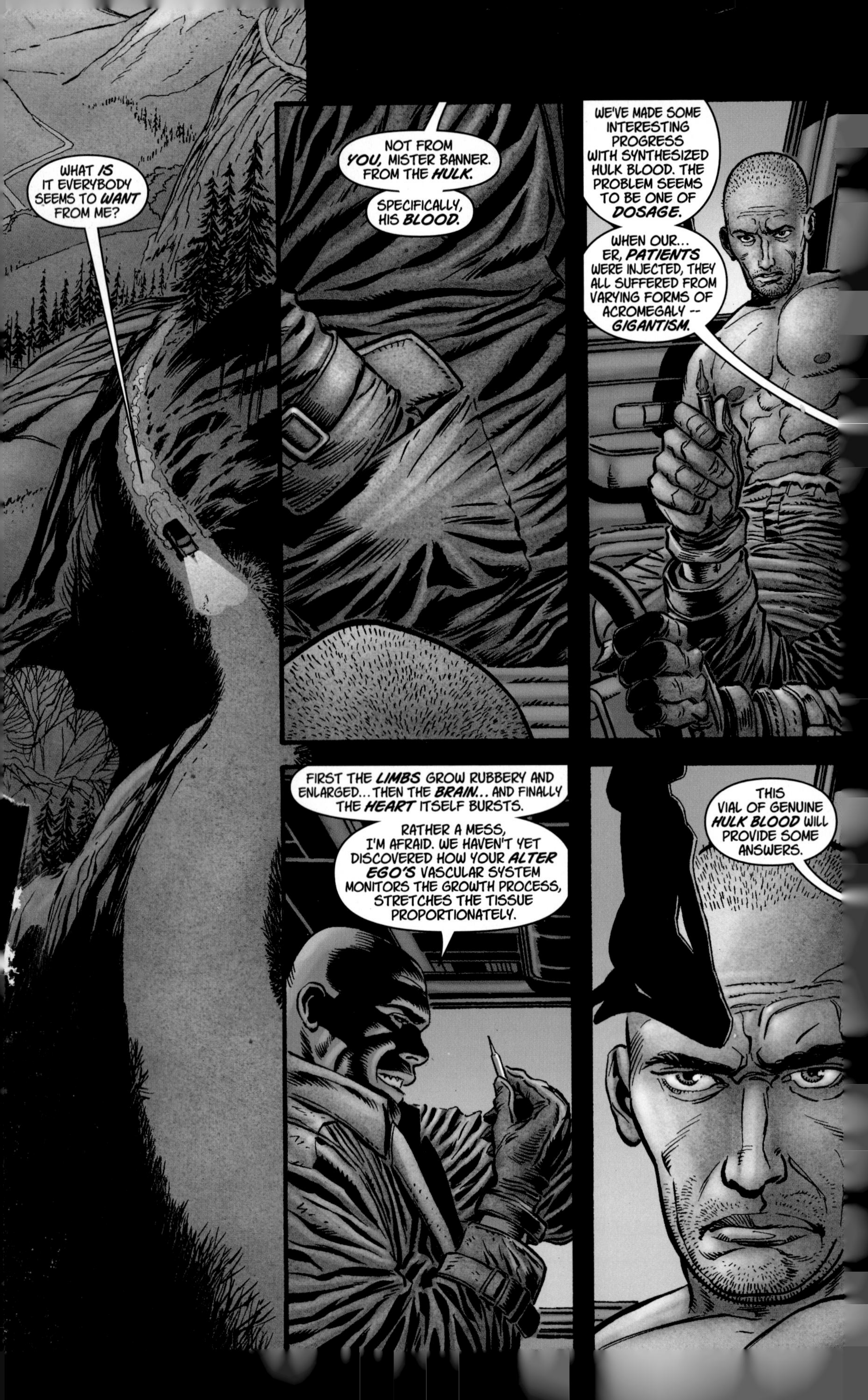
WHAT IS IT EVERYBODY SEEMS TO WANT FROM ME?
NOT FROM YOU, MISTER BANNER. FROM THE HULK.
SPECIFICALLY, HIS BLOOD.
WE'VE MADE SOME INTERESTING PROGRESS WITH SYNTHESIZED HULK BLOOD. THE PROBLEM SEEMS TO BE ONE OF DOSAGE.
WHEN OUR... ER, PATIENTS WERE INJECTED, THEY ALL SUFFERED FROM VARYING FORMS OF ACROMEGALY -- GIGANTISM.
FIRST THE LIMBS GROW RUBBERY AND ENLARGED... THEN THE BRAIN... AND FINALLY THE HEART ITSELF BURSTS.
RATHER A MESS, I'M AFRAID. WE HAVEN'T YET DISCOVERED HOW YOUR ALTER EGO'S VASCULAR SYSTEM MONITORS THE GROWTH PROCESS, STRETCHES THE TISSUE PROPORTIONATELY.
THIS VIAL OF GENUINE HULK BLOOD WILL PROVIDE SOME ANSWERS.

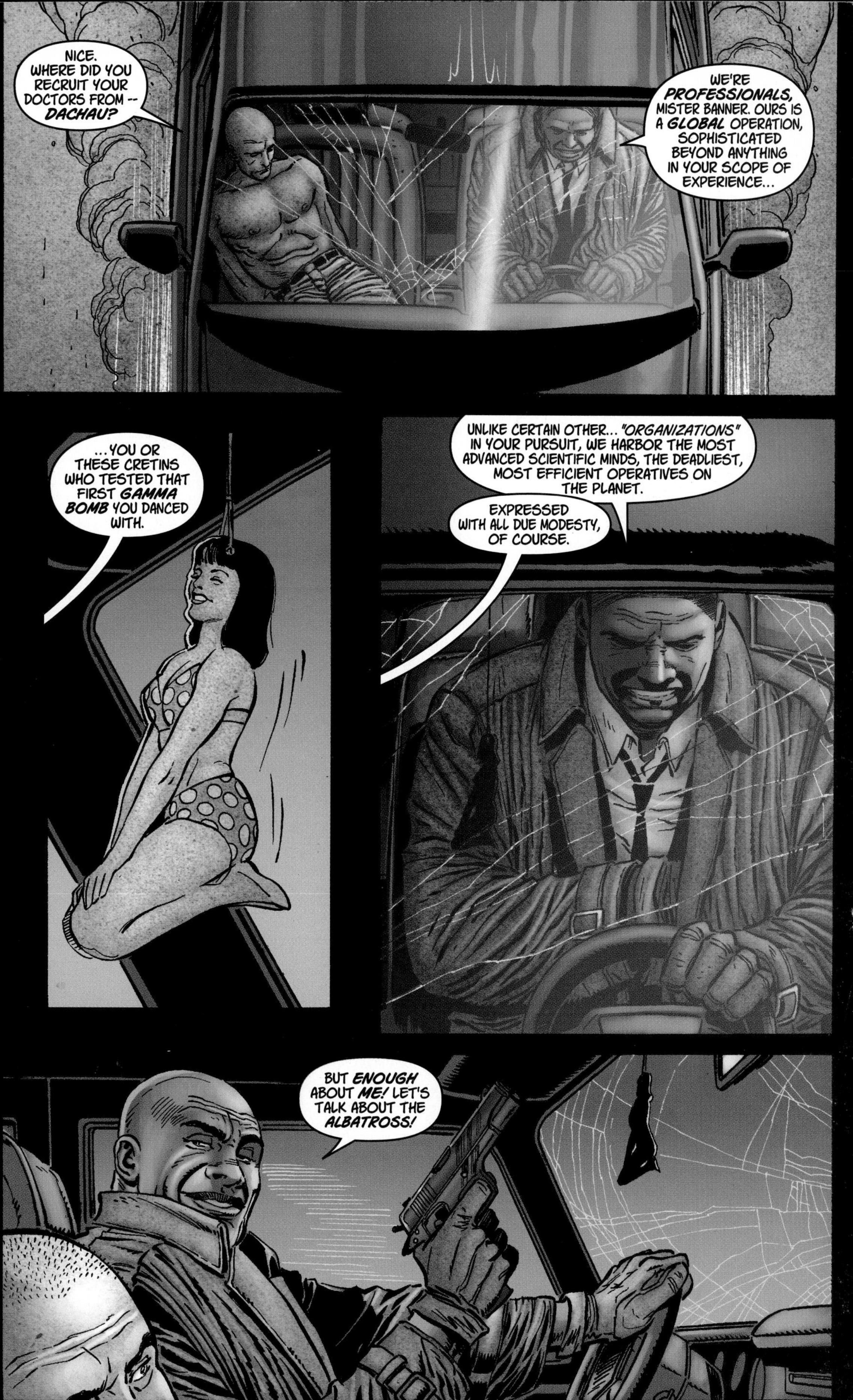
NICE. WHERE DID YOU RECRUIT YOUR DOCTORS FROM -- DACHAU?
WE'RE PROFESSIONALS, MISTER BANNER. OURS IS A GLOBAL OPERATION, SOPHISTICATED BEYOND ANYTHING IN YOUR SCOPE OF EXPERIENCE...
...YOU OR THESE CRETINS WHO TESTED THAT FIRST GAMMA BOMB YOU DANCED WITH.
UNLIKE CERTAIN OTHER... "ORGANIZATIONS" IN YOUR PURSUIT, WE HARBOR THE MOST ADVANCED SCIENTIFIC MINDS, THE DEADLIEST, MOST EFFICIENT OPERATIVES ON THE PLANET.
EXPRESSED WITH ALL DUE MODESTY, OF COURSE.
BUT ENOUGH ABOUT ME! LET'S TALK ABOUT THE ALBATROSS!

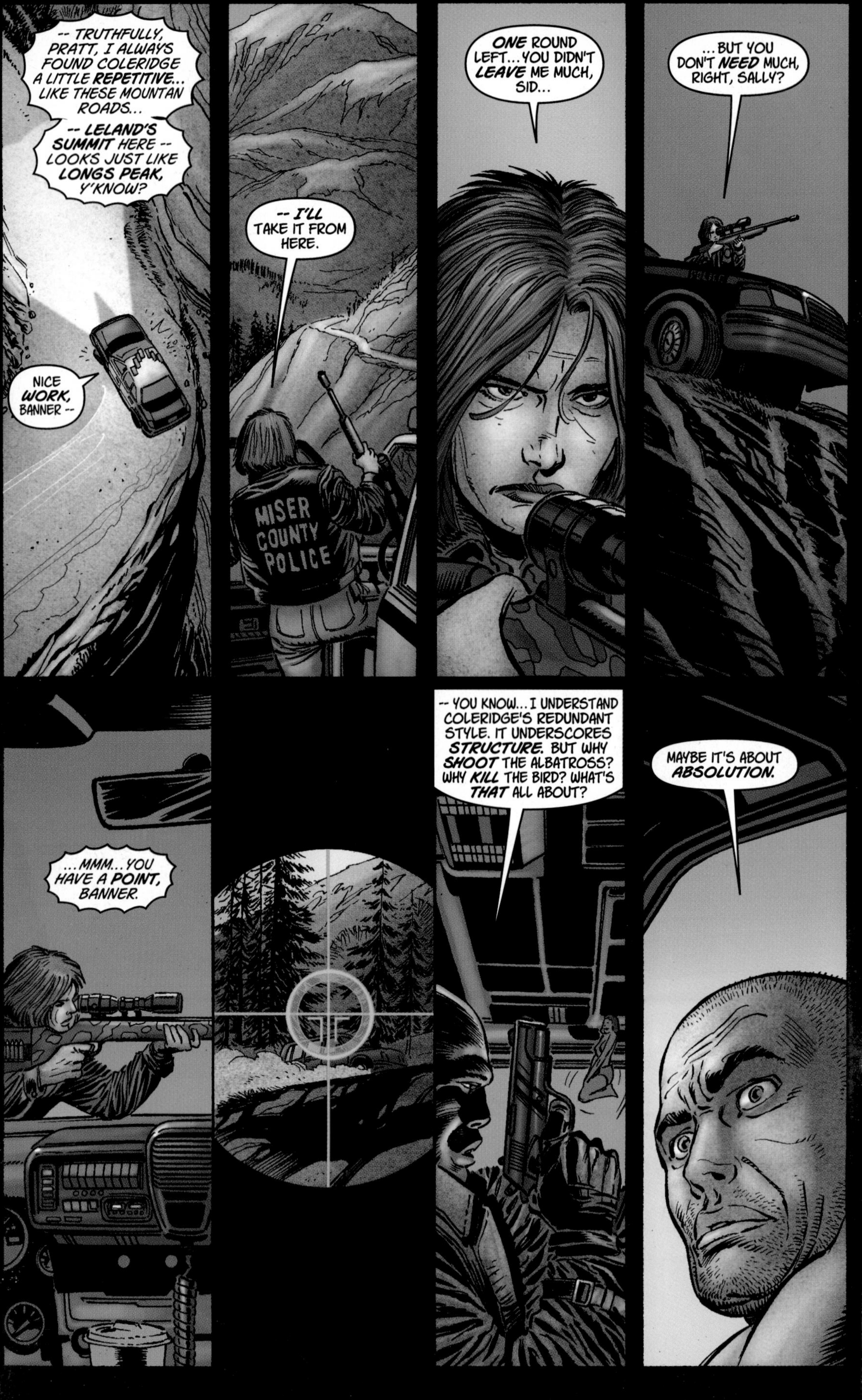
-- TRUTHFULLY, PRATT, I ALWAYS FOUND COLERIDGE A LITTLE REPETITIVE... LIKE THESE MOUNTAN ROADS...
-- LELAND'S SUMMIT HERE -- LOOKS JUST LIKE LONGS PEAK, Y'KNOW?
NICE WORK, BANNER --
-- I'LL TAKE IT FROM HERE.
MISER COUNTY POLICE
ONE ROUND LEFT... YOU DIDN'T LEAVE ME MUCH, SID...
... BUT YOU DON'T NEED MUCH, RIGHT, SALLY?
... MMM... YOU HAVE A POINT, BANNER.
-- YOU KNOW... I UNDERSTAND COLERIDGE'S REDUNDANT STYLE. IT UNDERSCORES STRUCTURE. BUT WHY SHOOT THE ALBATROSS? WHY KILL THE BIRD? WHAT'S THAT ALL ABOUT?
MAYBE IT'S ABOUT ABSOLUTION.

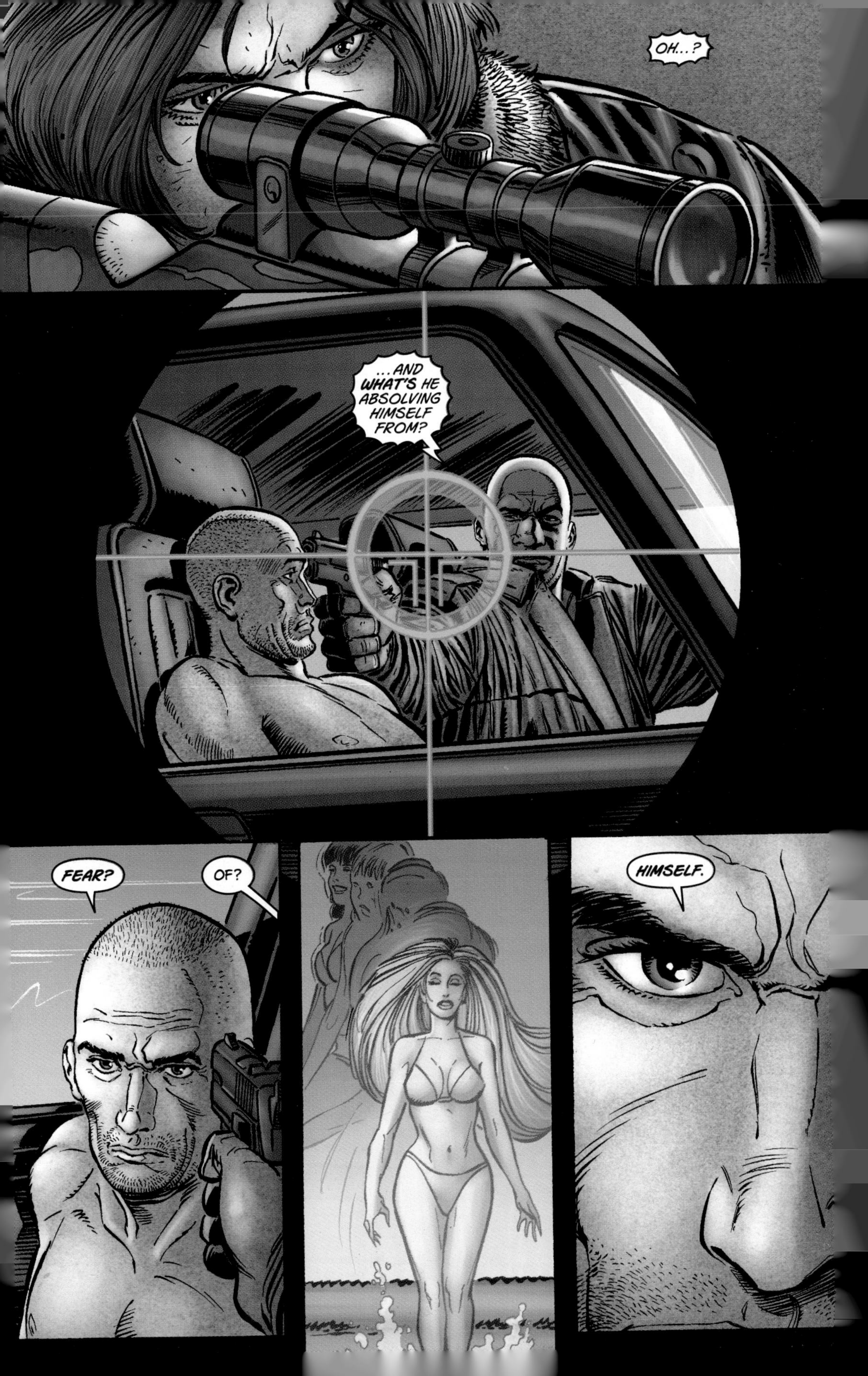
OH...?
...AND WHAT'S HE ABSOLVING HIMSELF FROM?
FEAR?
OF?
HIMSELF.

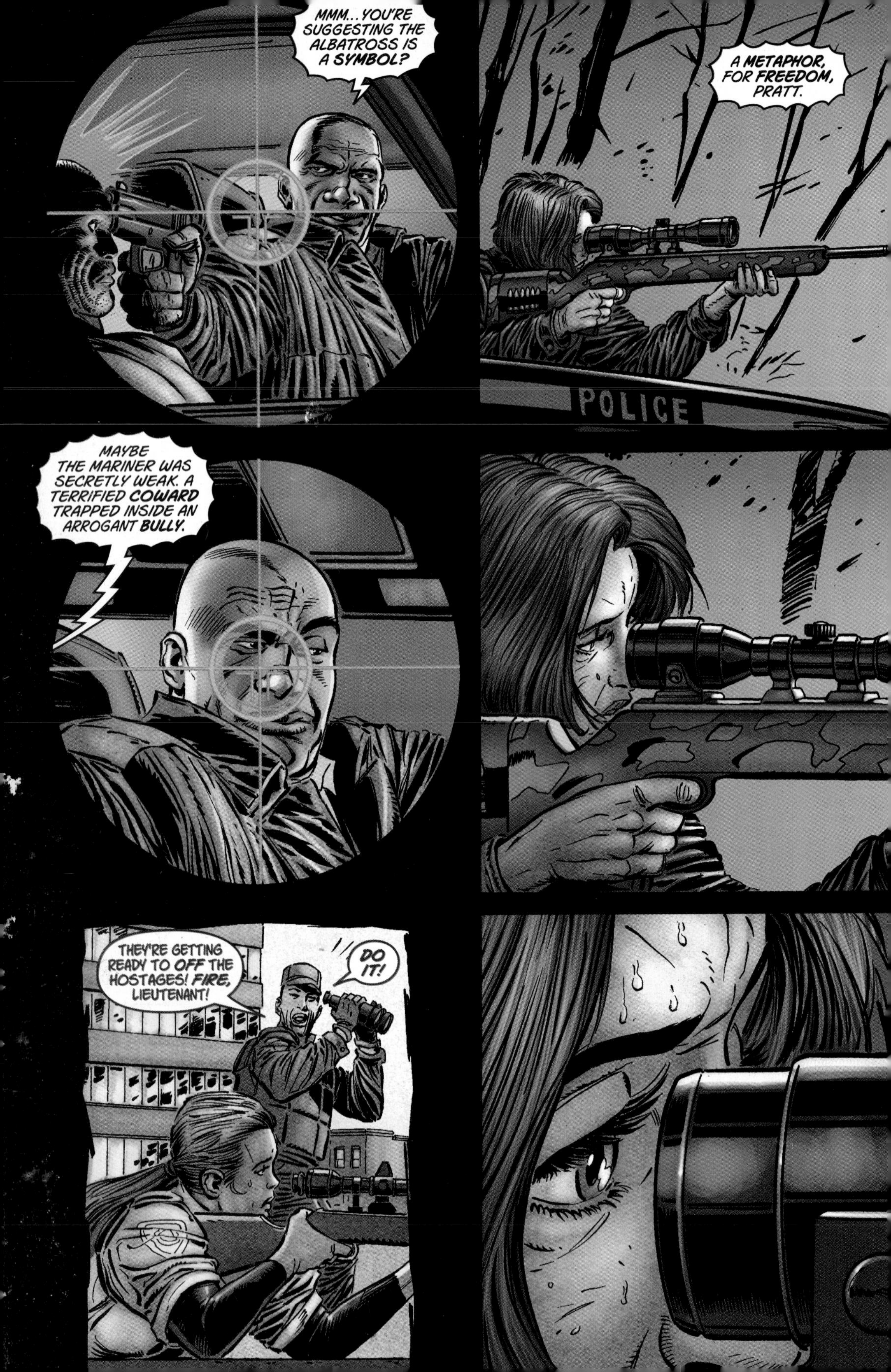
MMM...YOU'RE SUGGESTING THE ALBATROSS IS A SYMBOL?
A METAPHOR, FOR FREEDOM, PRATT.
POLICE
MAYBE THE MARINER WAS SECRETLY WEAK. A TERRIFIED COWARD TRAPPED INSIDE AN ARROGANT BULLY.
THEY'RE GETTING READY TO OFF THE HOSTAGES! FIRE, LIEUTENANT!
DO IT!

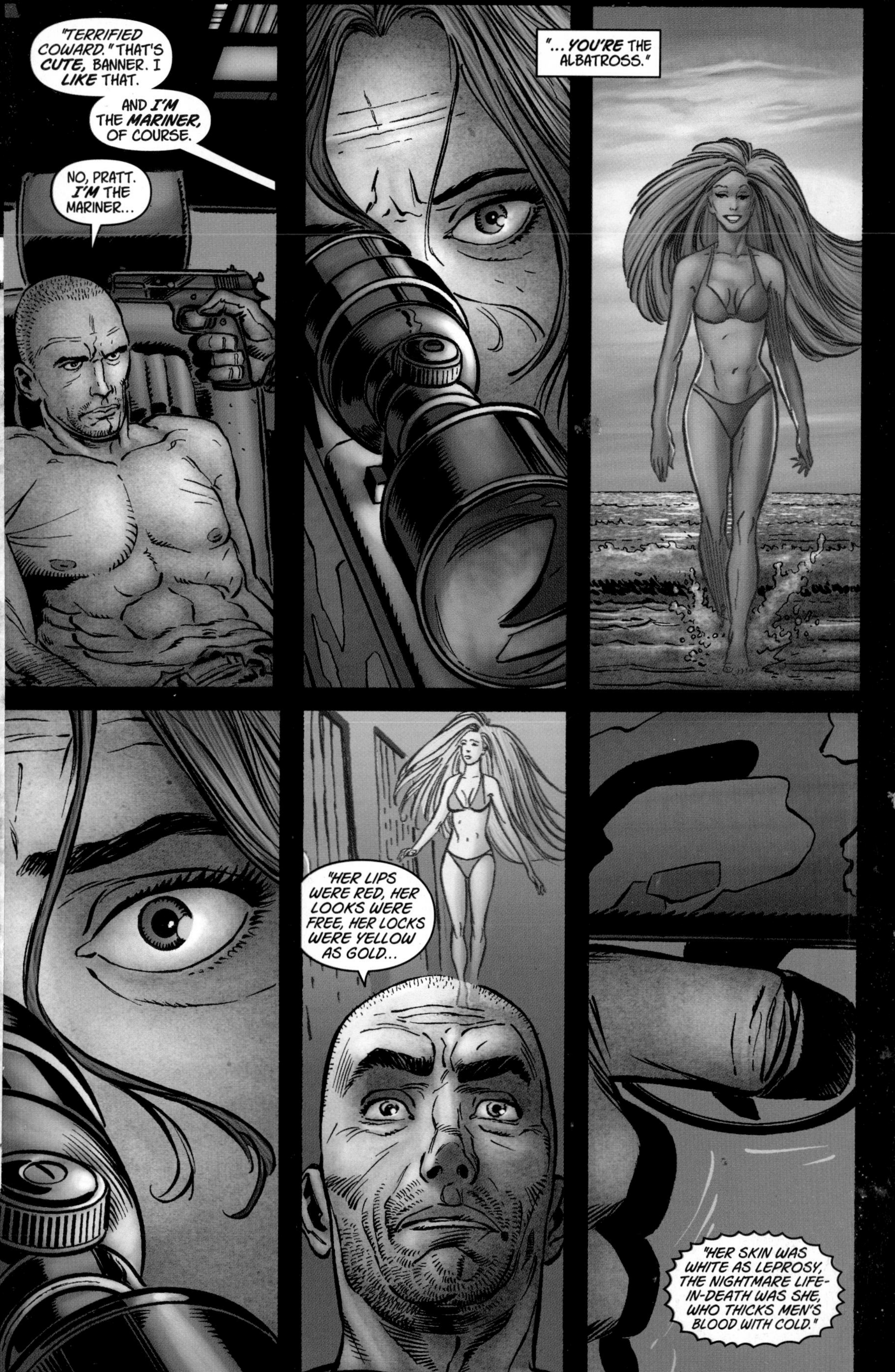
"TERRIFIED COWARD." THAT'S CUTE, BANNER. I LIKE THAT.
AND I'M THE MARINER, OF COURSE.
NO, PRATT. I'M THE MARINER...
"...YOU'RE THE ALBATROSS."
"HER LIPS WERE RED, HER LOOKS WERE FREE, HER LOCKS WERE YELLOW AS GOLD...
"HER SKIN WAS WHITE AS LEPROSY, THE NIGHTMARE LIFE-IN-DEATH WAS SHE, WHO THICKS MEN'S BLOOD WITH COLD."

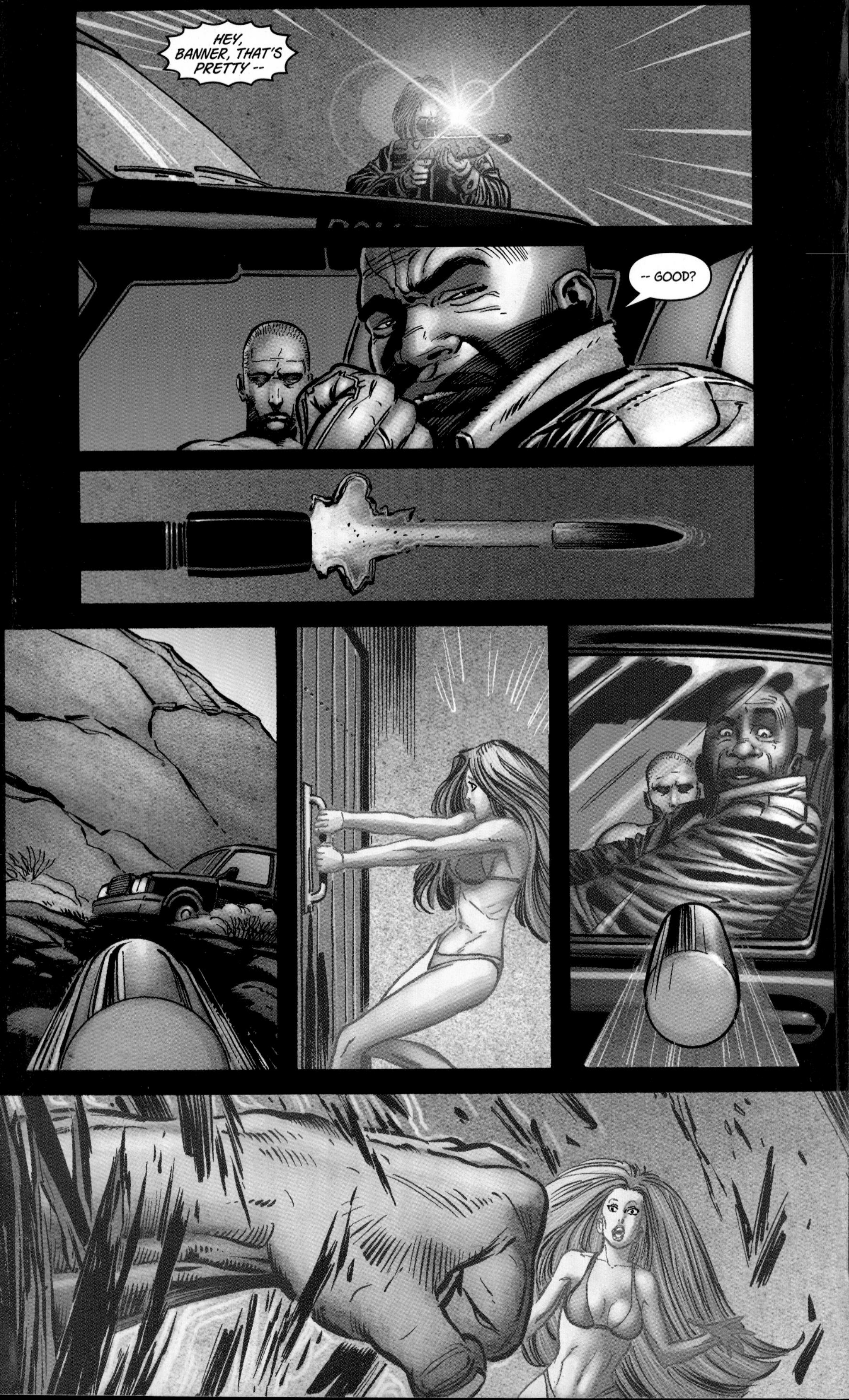
HEY, BANNER, THAT'S PRETTY --
-- GOOD?

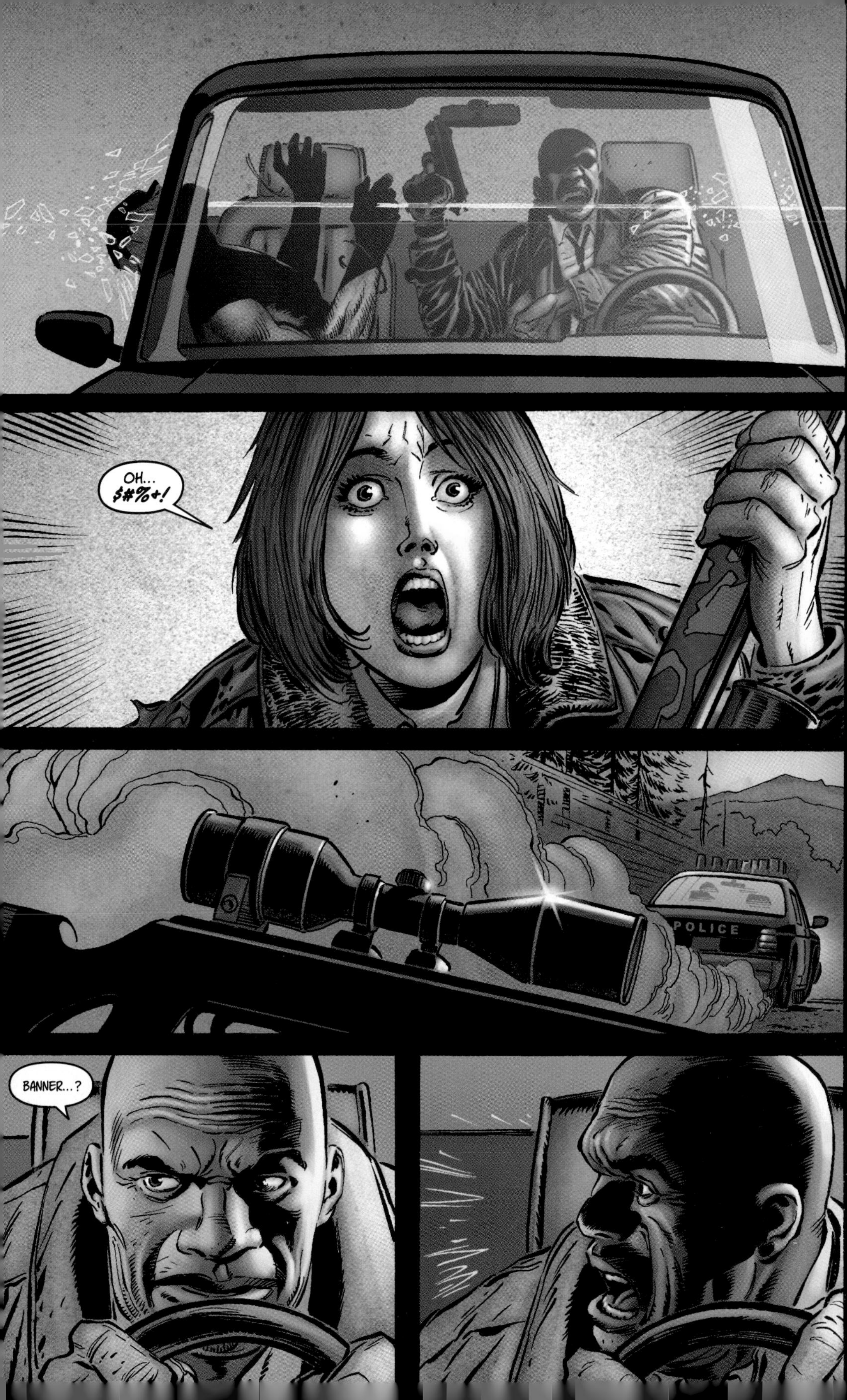
OH... $#%+!
POLICE
BANNER...?

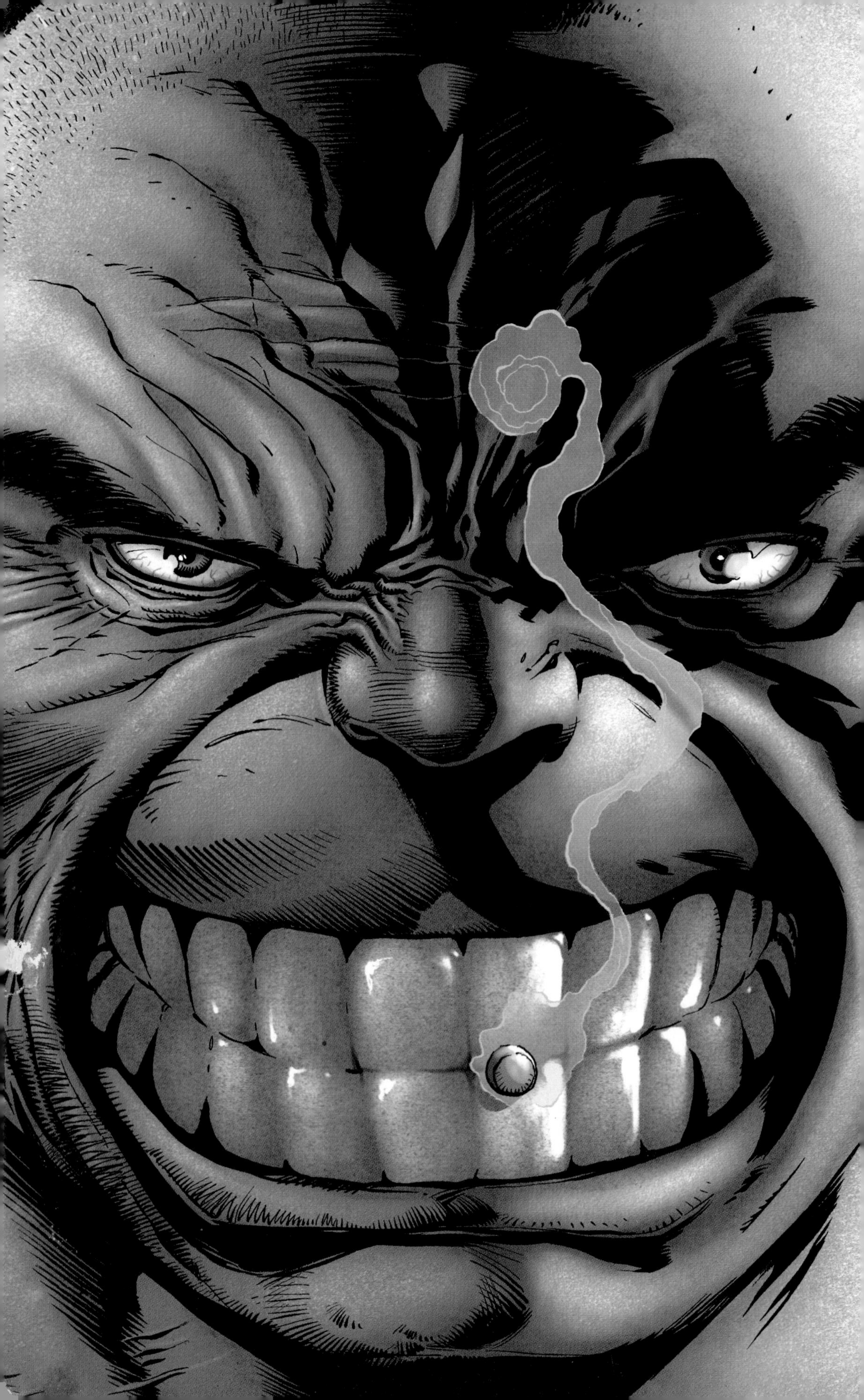

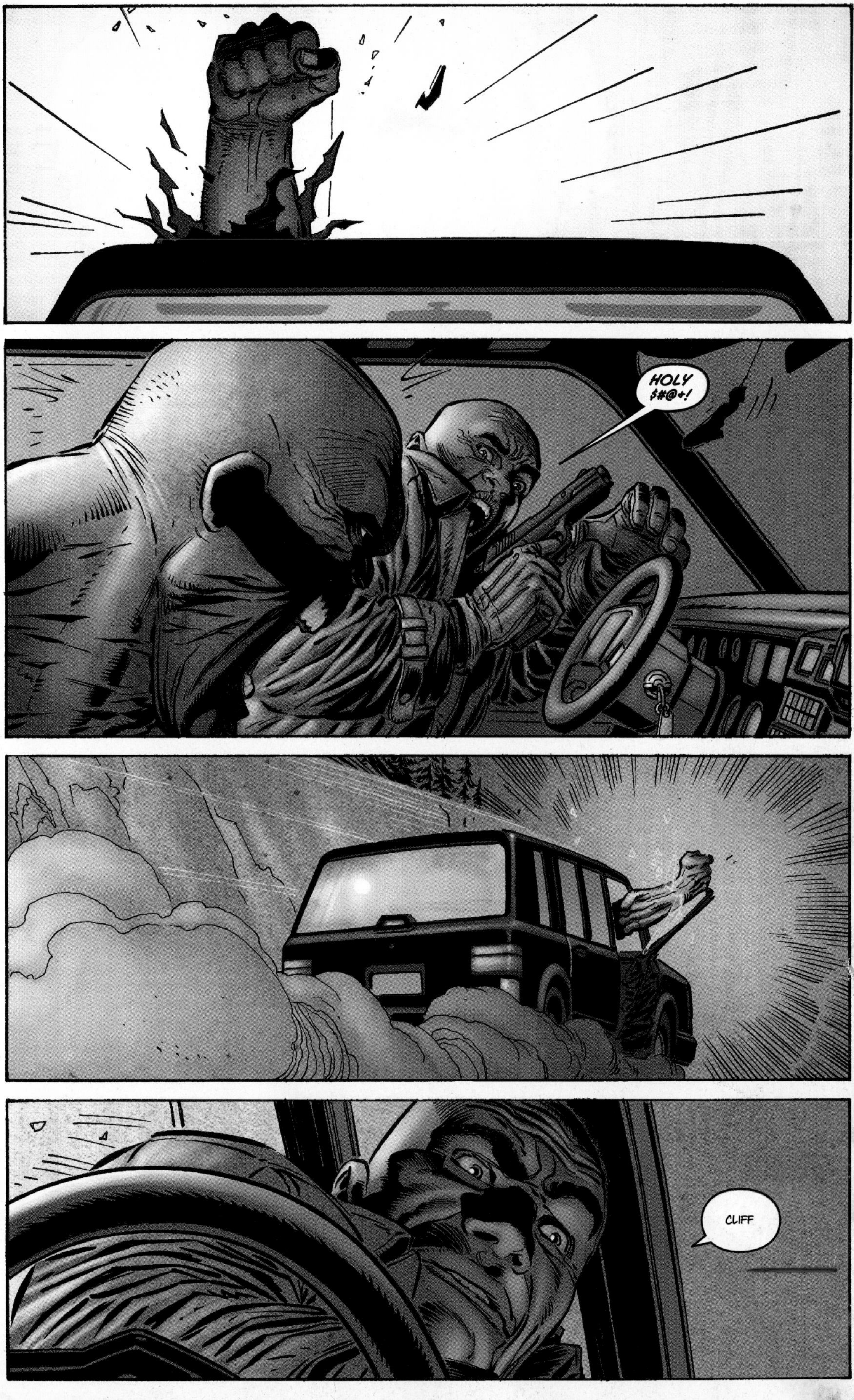
HOLY $#@+!
CLIFF

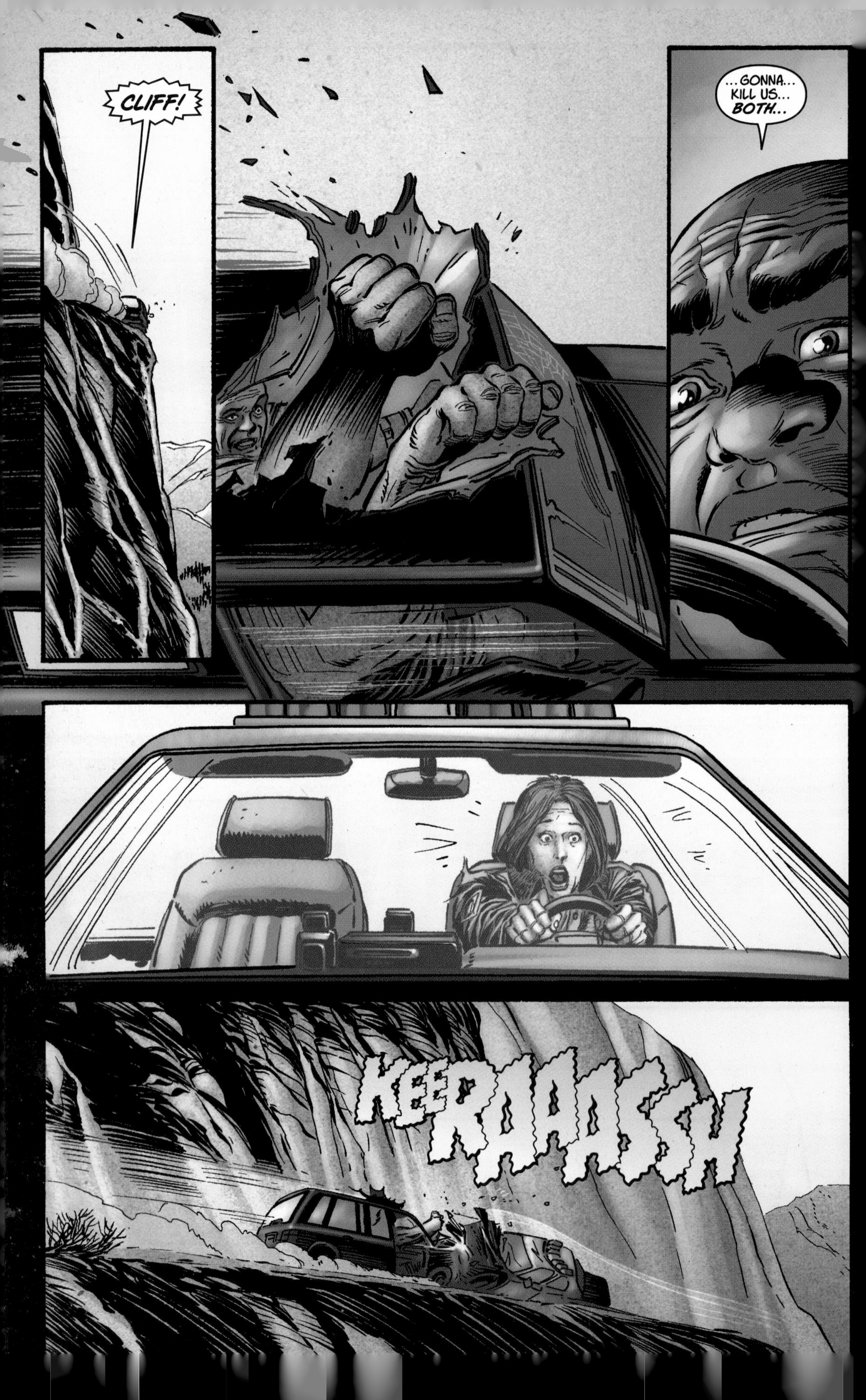
CLIFF!
...GONNA... KILL US... BOTH...
KEERAAASH

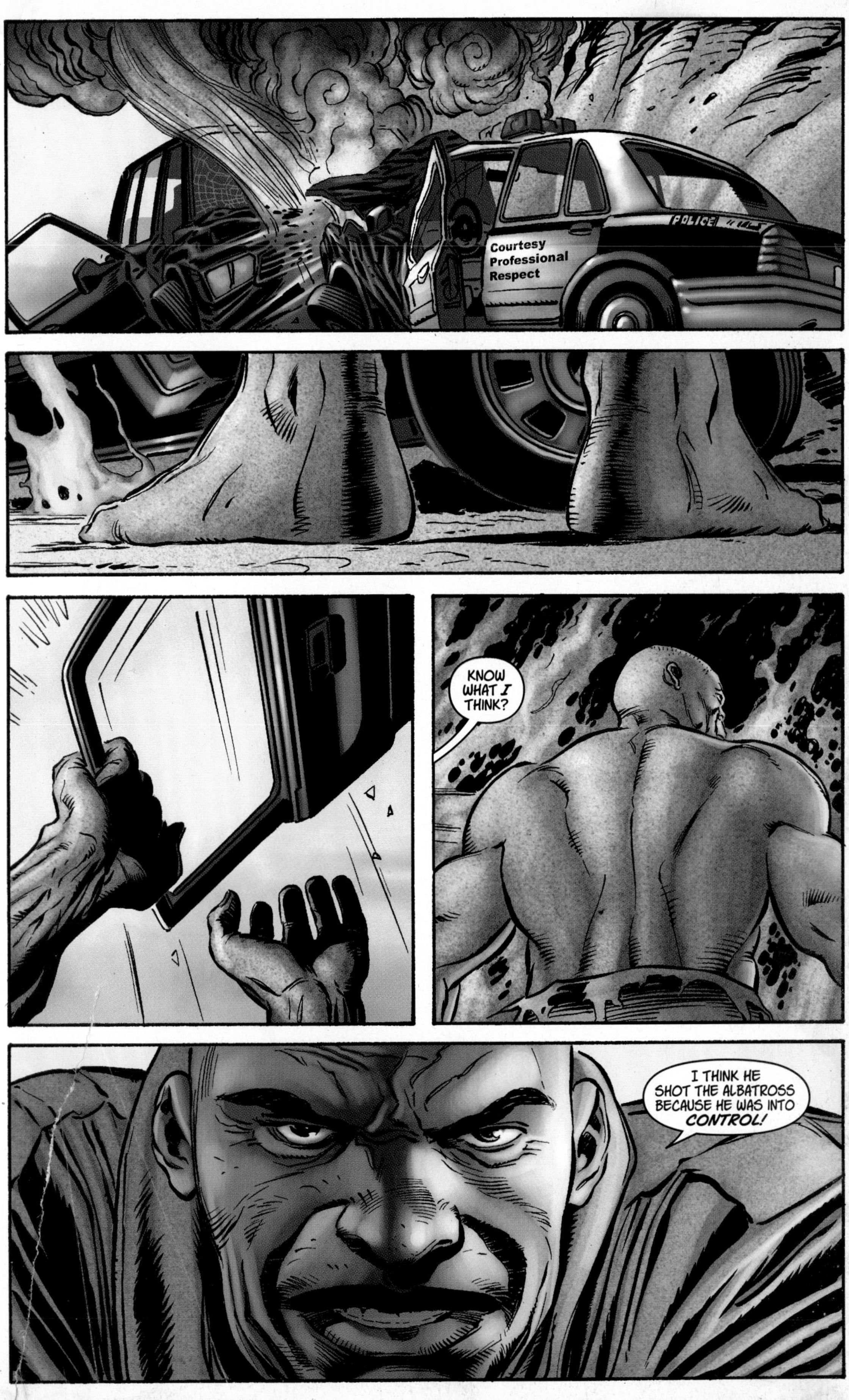
POLICE
Courtesy
Professional
Respect
KNOW WHAT I THINK?
I THINK HE SHOT THE ALBATROSS BECAUSE HE WAS INTO CONTROL!

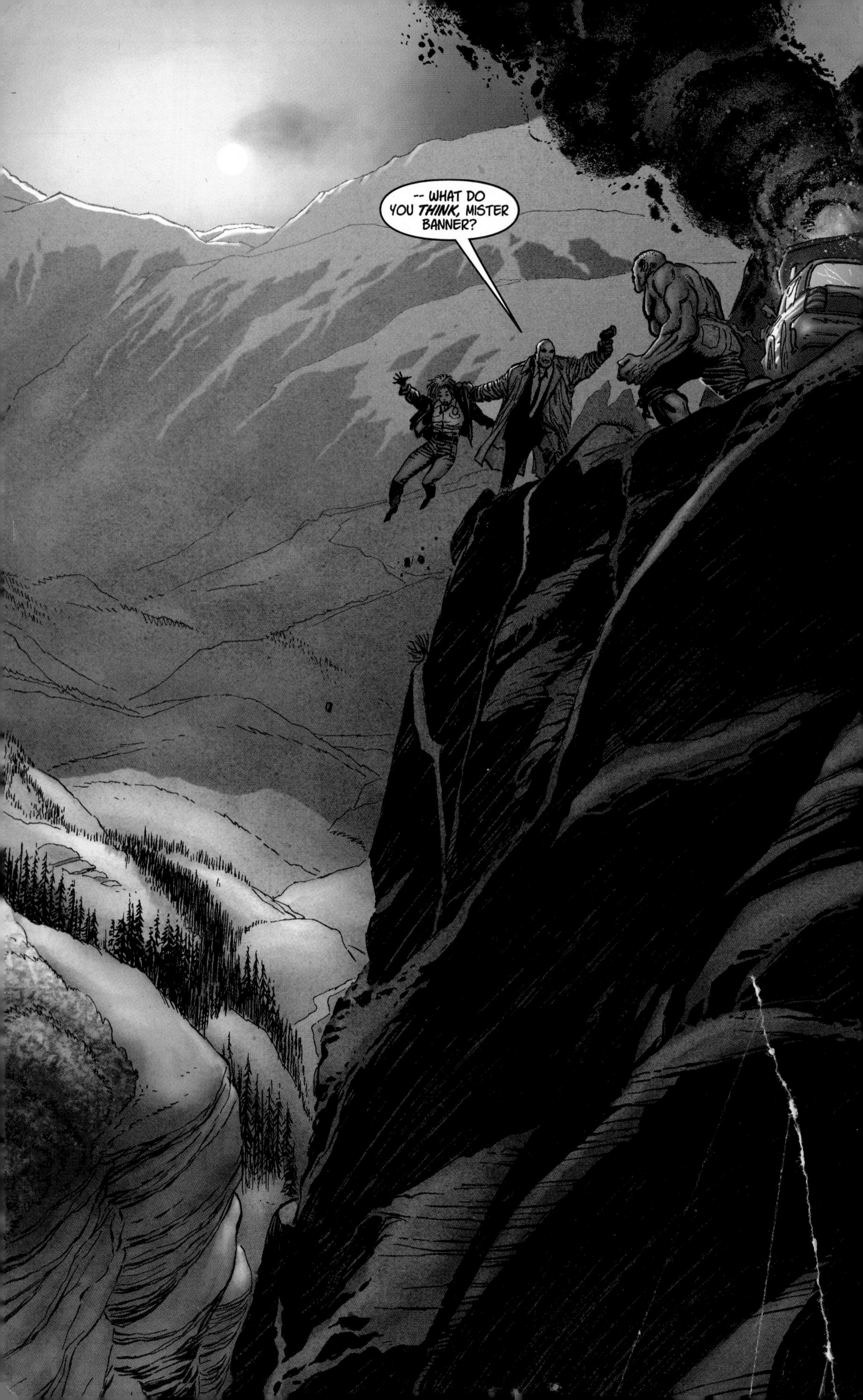
-- WHAT DO YOU THINK, MISTER BANNER?

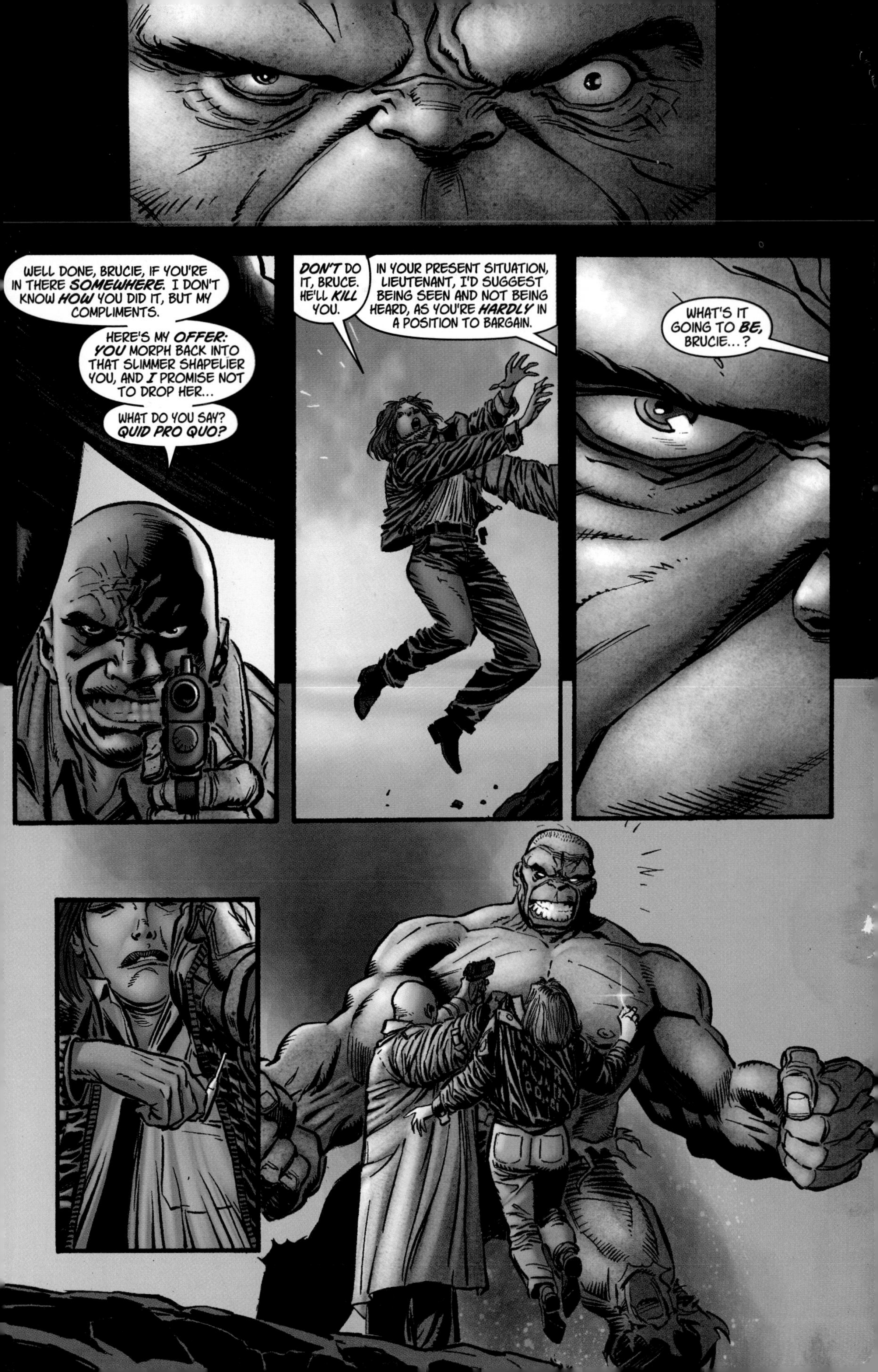
WELL DONE, BRUCIE, IF YOU'RE IN THERE SOMEWHERE. I DON'T KNOW HOW YOU DID IT, BUT MY COMPLIMENTS.
HERE'S MY OFFER: YOU MORPH BACK INTO THAT SLIMMER SHAPELIER YOU, AND I PROMISE NOT TO DROP HER...
WHAT DO YOU SAY? QUID PRO QUO?
DON'T DO IT, BRUCE. HE'LL KILL YOU.
IN YOUR PRESENT SITUATION, LIEUTENANT, I'D SUGGEST BEING SEEN AND NOT BEING HEARD, AS YOU'RE HARDLY IN A POSITION TO BARGAIN.
WHAT'S IT GOING TO BE, BRUCIE...?

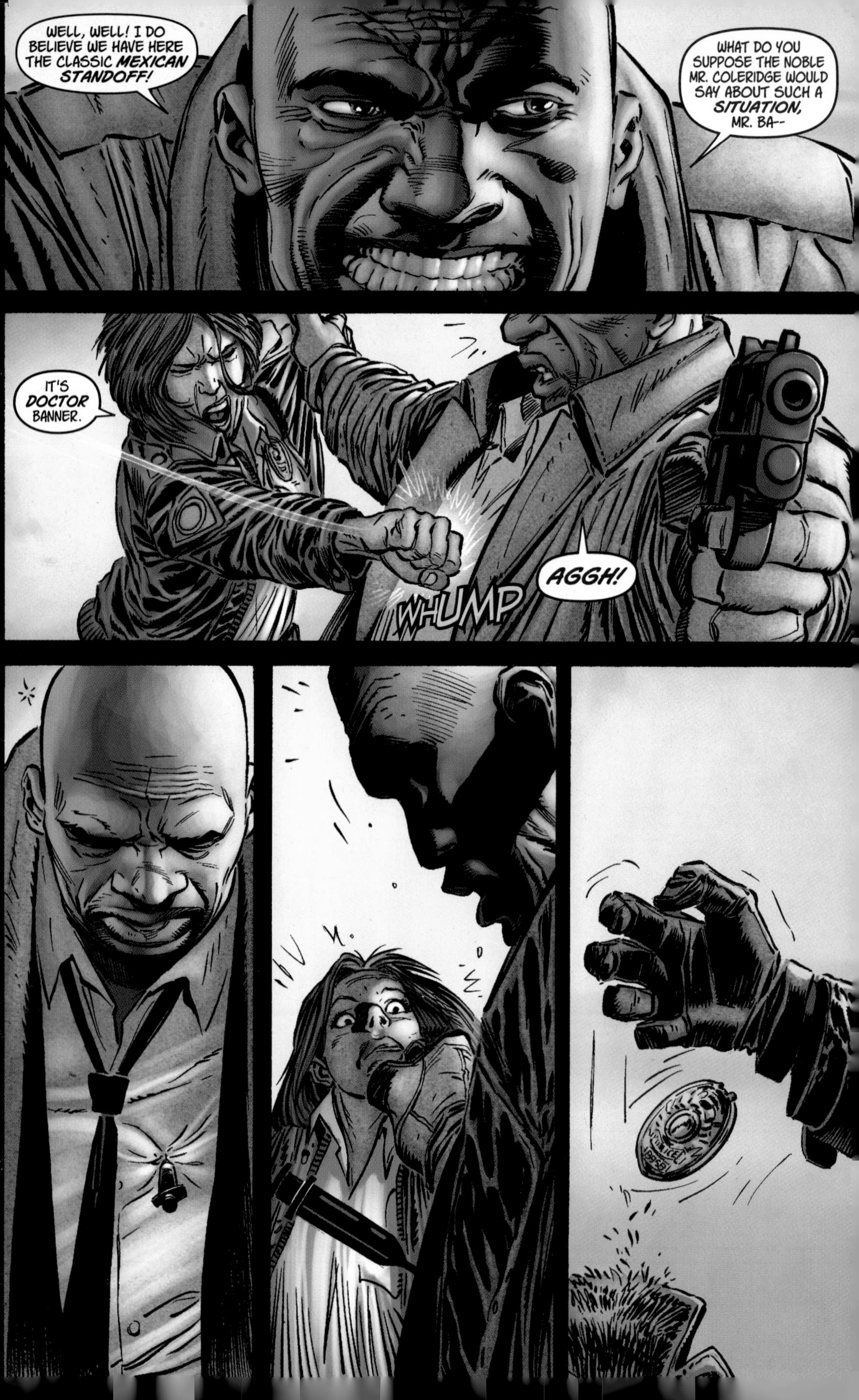
WELL, WELL! I DO BELIEVE WE HAVE HERE THE CLASSIC MEXICAN STANDOFF!
WHAT DO YOU SUPPOSE THE NOBLE MR. COLERIDGE WOULD SAY ABOUT SUCH A SITUATION, MR. BA--
IT'S DOCTOR BANNER.
WHUMP
AGGH!

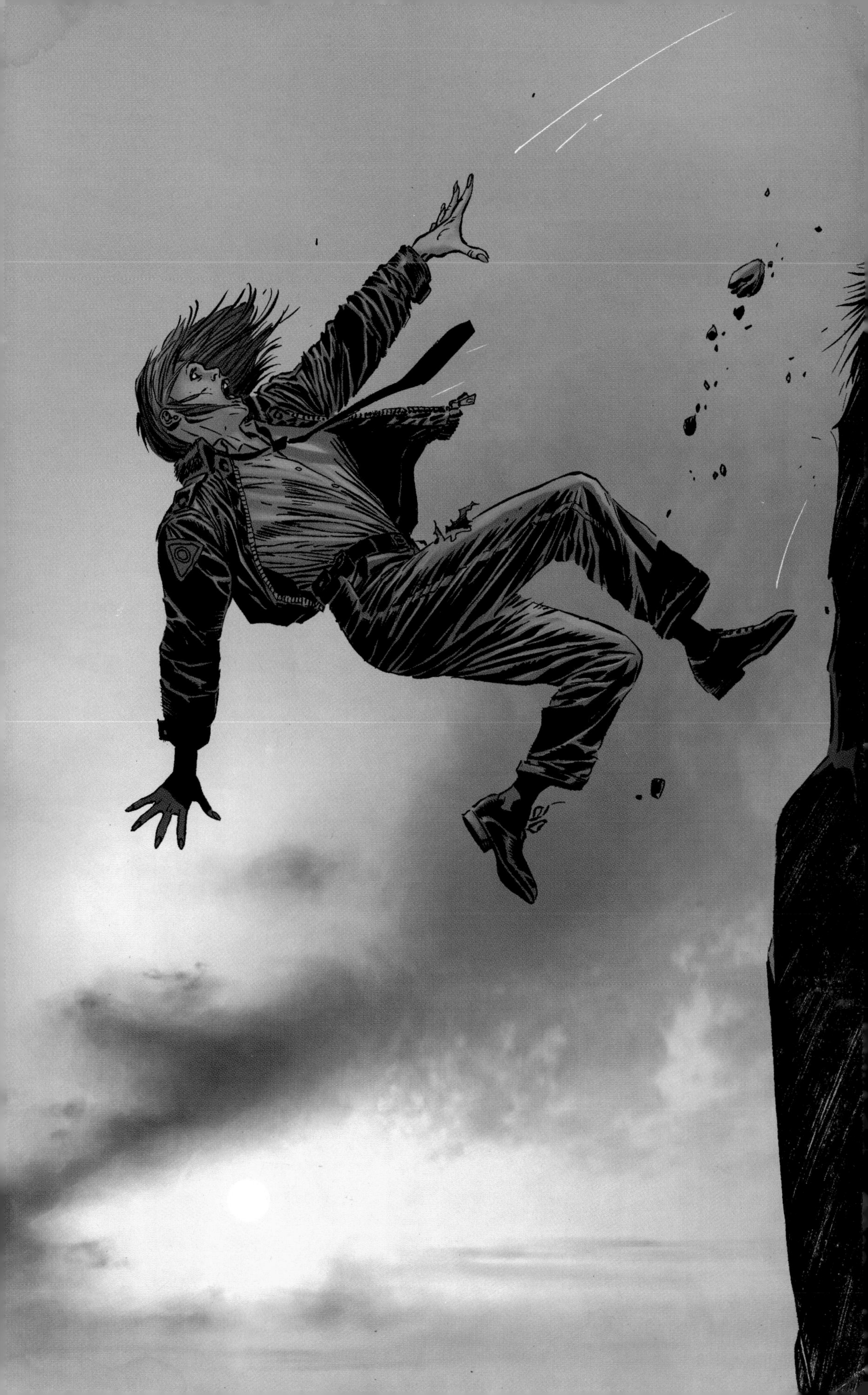

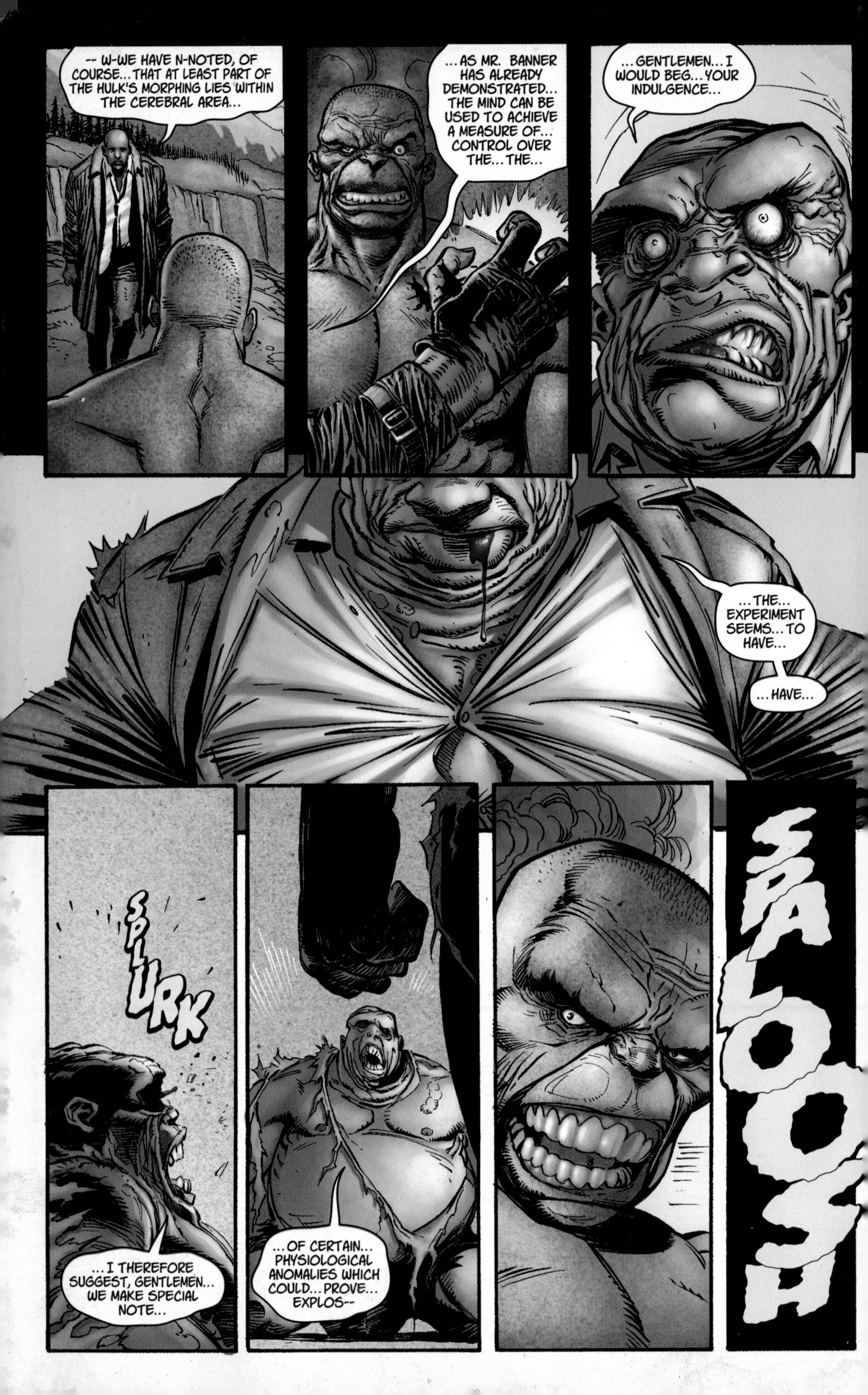
-- W-WE HAVE N-NOTED, OF COURSE... THAT AT LEAST PART OF THE HULK'S MORPHING LIES WITHIN THE CEREBRAL AREA...
...AS MR. BANNER HAS ALREADY DEMONSTRATED... THE MIND CAN BE USED TO ACHIEVE A MEASURE OF... CONTROL OVER THE... THE...
...GENTLEMEN... I WOULD BEG... YOUR INDULGENCE...
...THE... EXPERIMENT SEEMS... TO HAVE...
...HAVE...
SPLURK
...I THEREFORE SUGGEST, GENTLEMEN... WE MAKE SPECIAL NOTE...
...OF CERTAIN... PHYSIOLOGICAL ANOMALIES WHICH COULD... PROVE... EXPLOS--
SPALOOSH

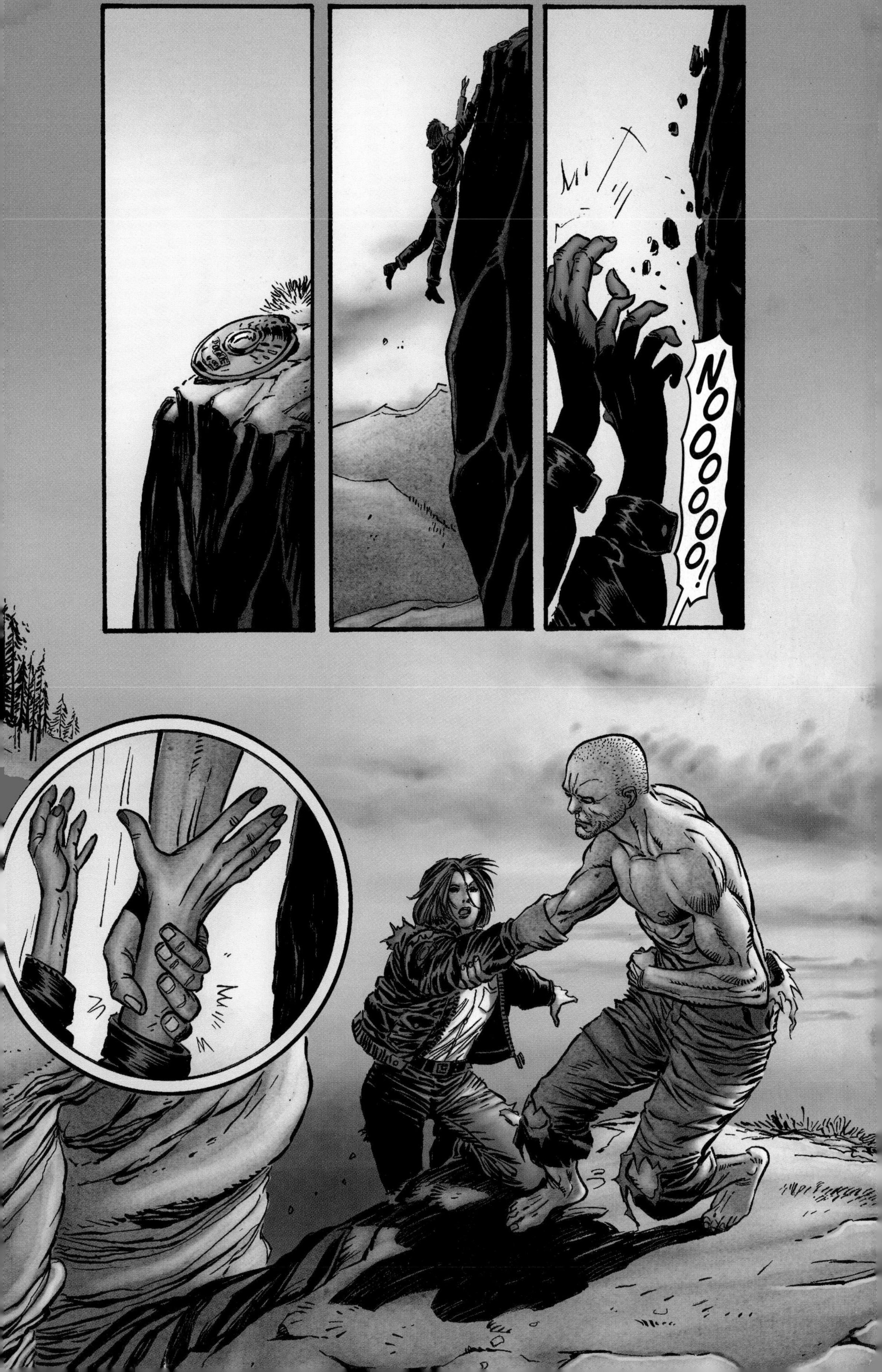
NOOOOOOO!

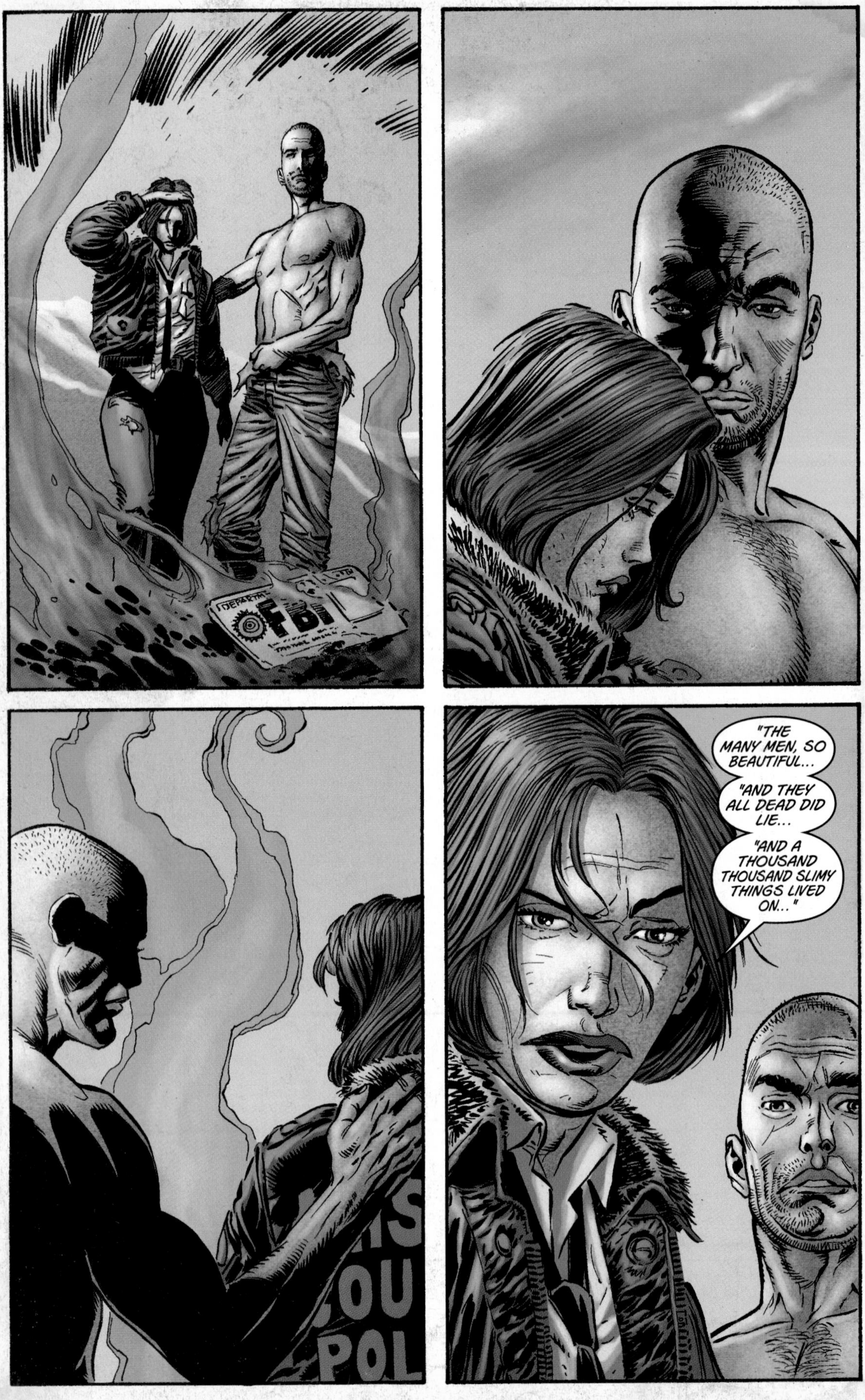
"THE MANY MEN, SO BEAUTIFUL...
"AND THEY ALL DEAD DID LIE...
"AND A THOUSAND THOUSAND SLIMY THINGS LIVED ON..."

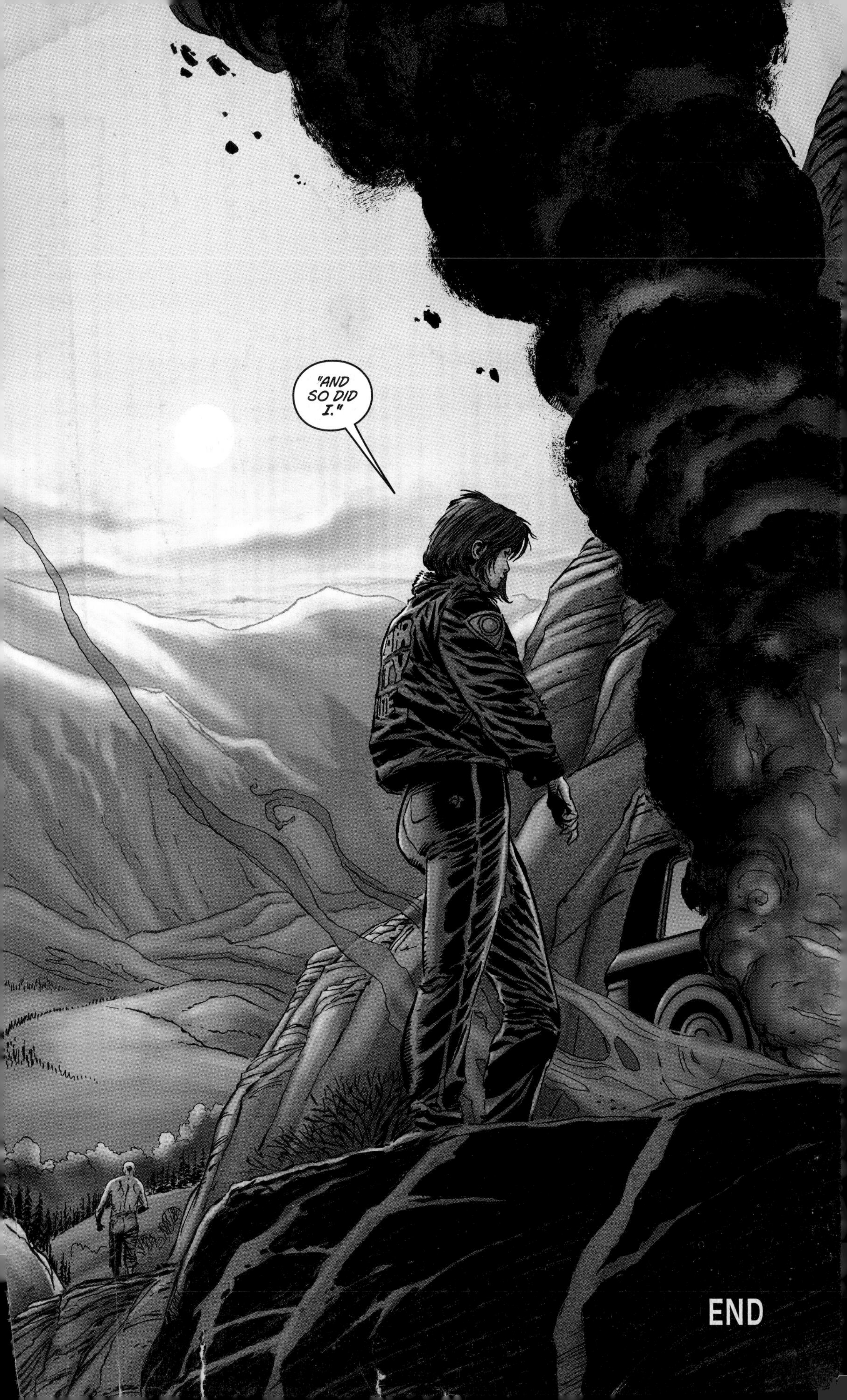
"AND SO DID I."
END

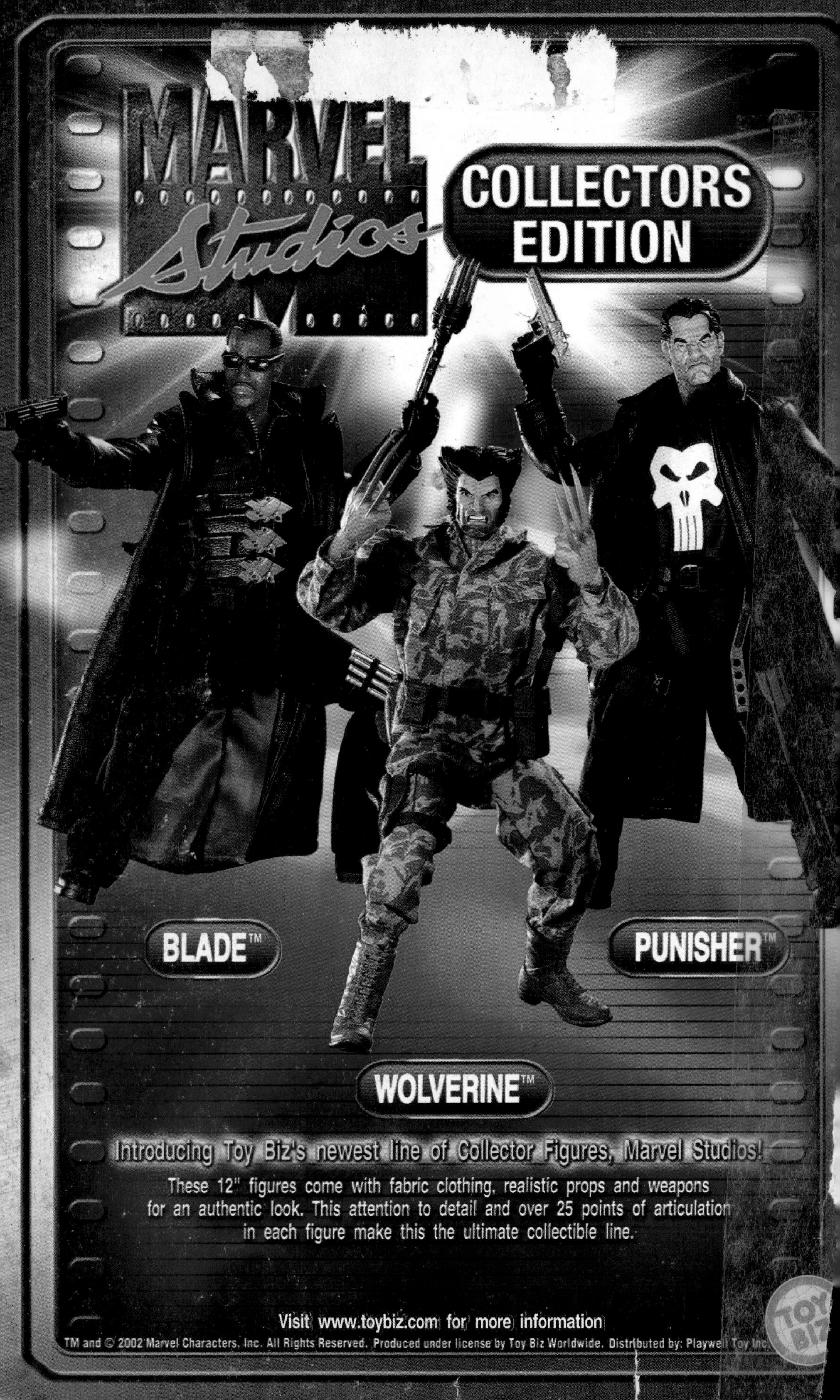
MARVEL Studios
COLLECTORS EDITION
BLADE™
PUNISHER™
WOLVERINE™
Introducing Toy Biz's newest line of Collector Figures, Marvel Studios!
These 12" figures come with fabric clothing, realistic props and weapons for an authentic look. This attention to detail and over 25 points of articulation in each figure make this the ultimate collectible line.
Visit www.toybiz.com for more information
TM and © 2002 Marvel Characters, Inc. All Rights Reserved. Produced under license by Toy Biz Worldwide. Distributed by: Playwell Toy Inc.
TOY BIZ